The Complete Ninja Foodi 2-Basket Air Fryer Cookbook

2100 Days of Simple, Quick, and Flavorful Recipes for Healthy and Crispy Meals with Effortless Dual-Zone Cooking

Julia Morgan

Table of Contents

Discover Your Exclusive Free Bonus!

Thank you for choosing "The Complete Ninja Foodi 2-Basket Air Fryer Cookbook"! We are excited to support your cooking adventures with three exclusive free bonus.

Scan the QR code to download these valuable resources:

Bonus 1: 15-Minute Meals

A collection of 50 quick and easy meals that can be made in 15 minutes or less, perfect for busy days.

Bonus 2: Tips for Cleaning and Maintaining Your Ninja Foodi

Learn the best practices for keeping your Ninja Foodi air fryer in top condition, ensuring it stays efficient and durable.

Bonus 3: Cooking for a Crowd with the Ninja Foodi

Discover strategies and recipes for preparing large meals using the dual-basket feature, ideal for gatherings and family dinners.

Don't miss out on these incredible bonus! Scan the QR code to download your free resources and make the most of your Ninja Foodi cooking experience. Happy cooking!

Introduction

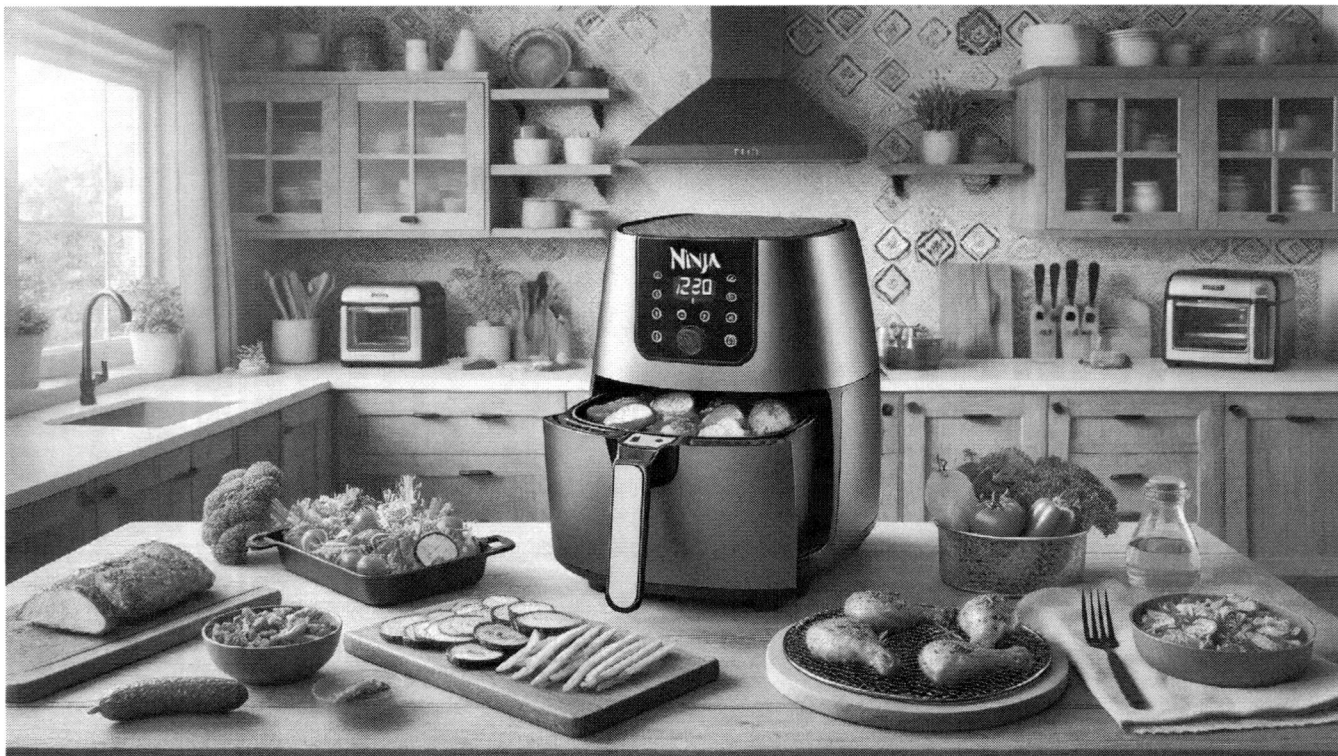

Meet Your Ninja Foodi 2-Basket Air Fryer: A Game-Changer in Your Kitchen

Welcome to the world of effortless cooking with the Ninja Foodi 2-Basket Air Fryer! Whether you're a busy parent trying to get dinner on the table quickly or a culinary enthusiast looking to explore new cooking techniques, this appliance is about to become your best friend in the kitchen. The Ninja Foodi 2-Basket Air Fryer isn't just another kitchen gadget—it's a revolutionary tool designed to simplify your cooking routine while delivering delicious, healthy meals with minimal effort.

What sets the Ninja Foodi 2-Basket Air Fryer apart from traditional air fryers is its innovative DualZone technology. Imagine being able to cook two different foods at the same time, with separate temperature and timing controls, all within one compact appliance. No more juggling multiple pans on the stove or worrying about dishes getting cold while you wait for another to finish. With the Ninja Foodi, you can prepare a perfectly crispy chicken breast in one basket while simultaneously roasting vegetables in the other. The result? A complete, balanced meal with less fuss and more flavor.

This air fryer isn't just about convenience; it's about empowering you to make healthier choices without sacrificing taste. By using hot air circulation to cook food, the Ninja Foodi achieves that coveted crispy texture with up to 75% less oil than traditional frying methods. That means you can enjoy your favorite fried foods—think French fries, chicken wings, and even doughnuts—without the guilt. Plus, the dual-basket design makes it easier than ever to prepare meals for the whole family, even when everyone has different dietary preferences or restrictions.

How to Use This Cookbook for Maximum Results

This cookbook is designed to help you unlock the full potential of your Ninja Foodi 2-Basket Air Fryer, whether you're a novice in the kitchen or an experienced cook. Each section is carefully crafted to guide you through the process of mastering your air fryer, with recipes that cater to a wide range of tastes and dietary needs. From quick breakfasts and lunches to hearty dinners and indulgent desserts, you'll find a variety of recipes that are easy to follow and even easier to enjoy.

To get the most out of this cookbook, I recommend starting with the basics in Section 1. Here, you'll find everything you need to know about setting up your Ninja Foodi, understanding its functions, and learning the science behind air frying. This foundational knowledge will set you up for success as you explore the recipes in Section 2, which are organized by meal type and ingredient. Whether you're in the mood for a quick snack, a plant-based meal, or a family-friendly dinner, you'll find plenty of options to choose from.

Each recipe includes step-by-step instructions, complete with cooking times and temperature settings tailored specifically for the Ninja Foodi 2-Basket Air Fryer. You'll also find helpful tips and variations to customize the recipes to your taste or dietary preferences. If you're new to air frying, don't worry—I've included essential tips and troubleshooting advice to help you avoid common pitfalls and achieve perfect results every time.

Understanding DualZone Technology and Its Benefits

At the heart of the Ninja Foodi 2-Basket Air Fryer is the DualZone technology, which is a game-changer for home cooks. This feature allows you to cook two different foods simultaneously, each with its own temperature and time settings. The beauty of DualZone technology is its flexibility. You can choose to SyncCook, where both baskets cook the same food at the same settings, or SyncFinish, where two different foods finish cooking at the same time, even if they require different temperatures and cooking durations.

Imagine preparing a full meal without the stress of timing everything perfectly. With SyncFinish, you can cook a protein in one basket and a side dish in the other, ensuring they are both ready to serve at the same time. For example, you could cook a piece of salmon at 400°F (200°C) for 12 minutes in one basket while roasting asparagus at 375°F (190°C) for 10 minutes in the other. The Ninja Foodi will automatically adjust the timing so that both dishes are ready simultaneously.

This technology also opens up endless possibilities for meal planning and preparation. You can batch-cook different components of your meals in one go, reducing the time you spend in the kitchen and minimizing cleanup. Whether you're cooking for one, two, or a family, the Ninja Foodi 2-Basket Air Fryer adapts to your needs, making it an invaluable tool for anyone looking to streamline their cooking process.

Essential Tips for Air Frying Success

Air frying with the Ninja Foodi 2-Basket Air Fryer is straightforward, but there are a few key tips to ensure you get the best results every time. These tips will help you avoid common mistakes and make the most of your air frying experience.

1. **Preheat When Necessary**: While the Ninja Foodi preheats quickly, it's often beneficial to preheat the air fryer before adding your food, especially for recipes that require a crispy exterior. Preheating helps the food start cooking immediately, resulting in better texture and even cooking. Most recipes will specify if preheating is required.

2. **Don't Overcrowd the Baskets**: Air fryers work by circulating hot air around the food, so it's important not to overcrowd the baskets. If the food is too packed, the air can't circulate properly, leading to uneven cooking and less crispy results. For best results, arrange food in a single layer with a bit of space between pieces. If you're cooking for a crowd, consider cooking in batches.

3. **Shake or Flip Halfway Through**: For foods like fries, chicken wings, or vegetables, shaking the basket or flipping the food halfway through the cooking time ensures even browning on all sides. This simple step can make a big difference in the texture of your food.

4. **Use the Right Temperature and Time**: Different foods require different temperatures and cooking times to achieve the best results. Higher temperatures are great for crispy exteriors, while lower temperatures are better for cooking food through without burning. This cookbook provides specific temperature and time settings for each recipe, so be sure to follow them closely.

5. **Experiment with Seasonings**: One of the joys of air frying is that it enhances the flavors of your food. Don't be afraid to experiment with different seasonings and marinades to find what you like best. Just remember that a little goes a long way, especially with spices and herbs.

6. **Use Oil Sparingly**: One of the biggest benefits of air frying is that it requires much less oil than traditional frying methods. However, a small amount of oil can still help achieve that perfect golden-brown finish. Use a light spray of cooking oil or brush a small amount of oil on your food before cooking. Be sure to use oils with a high smoke point, like avocado oil or olive oil, for the best results.

7. **Clean Your Air Fryer Regularly**: Regular cleaning is essential to keep your air fryer in good working condition and to prevent any unwanted flavors from lingering. After each use, be sure to clean the baskets, crisper plates, and any other removable parts with warm, soapy water. For a deeper clean, wipe down the inside of the air fryer with a damp cloth. Avoid using abrasive sponges or harsh cleaners that could damage the non-stick coating.

The Health Benefits of Air Frying: Less Oil, More Flavor

One of the main reasons air fryers have become so popular is their ability to create crispy, delicious food with significantly less oil than traditional frying methods. This not only reduces the calorie content of your meals but also makes them healthier by cutting down on the amount of unhealthy fats you consume.

When you fry food in oil, it absorbs a significant amount of fat, which can contribute to high cholesterol levels, weight gain, and other health issues. Air frying, on the other hand, uses hot air to cook the food, requiring only a fraction of the oil. This means you can still enjoy your favorite fried foods—like French fries, chicken wings, and mozzarella sticks—without the excess grease and calories.

In addition to reducing fat intake, air frying also helps preserve the nutrients in your food. Traditional frying methods can destroy some of the vitamins and minerals in food due to the high temperatures and prolonged cooking times. Air frying, with its shorter cooking times and lower temperatures, helps retain more of these essential nutrients, making your meals not only tastier but also more nutritious.

Moreover, air frying reduces the risk of harmful compounds like acrylamide, which can form when starchy foods are fried at high temperatures. Studies have shown that air frying significantly lowers the formation of acrylamide compared to deep frying, making it a safer option for enjoying crispy foods.

By using your Ninja Foodi 2-Basket Air Fryer, you're not just making healthier choices for yourself; you're also contributing to the well-being of your family. The versatility of this appliance allows you to prepare a wide range of meals that cater to different dietary preferences and restrictions, all while maintaining the delicious flavors and textures that make food enjoyable.

As you explore the recipes in this cookbook, you'll discover that healthy eating doesn't have to be boring or time-consuming. With the Ninja Foodi 2-Basket Air Fryer, you can whip up everything from crispy vegetables to tender meats, all with minimal oil and maximum flavor. Whether you're looking to lose weight, manage a health condition, or simply eat better, air frying is a fantastic way to achieve your goals without feeling deprived.

In the chapters that follow, you'll find a variety of recipes that demonstrate just how versatile and easy-to-use the Ninja Foodi 2-Basket Air Fryer can be. From quick breakfasts to hearty dinners, this cookbook will guide you through the process of creating healthy, delicious meals that your whole family will love. So let's get started on this exciting culinary journey together—your Ninja Foodi is waiting!

Section 1: Mastering the Basics

Chapter 1: Getting Started with Your Ninja Foodi

Unboxing and Setup: What You Need to Know

Congratulations on your purchase of the Ninja Foodi 2-Basket Air Fryer! You're about to embark on a culinary journey that will not only save you time in the kitchen but also allow you to prepare delicious and healthier meals for yourself and your loved ones. The Ninja Foodi is a powerful, versatile appliance that may seem a bit intimidating at first, but don't worry—I'm here to guide you through every step.

When you first unbox your Ninja Foodi, you'll find a few key components that are essential for your cooking experience. Inside the box, you should see:

1. **The Main Unit**: This is the body of the air fryer, which houses the control panel, heating elements, and fan system that powers the cooking process.

2. **Two Baskets**: These are the heart of the DualZone technology, allowing you to cook two different foods simultaneously.

3. **Crisper Plates**: These go inside the baskets and help to circulate air around the food, ensuring that everything cooks evenly and crisps up nicely.

4. **Instruction Manual and Recipe Booklet**: While this book will provide you with plenty of recipes, it's always good to glance through the manual to familiarize yourself with the appliance.

Before you start cooking, it's important to properly set up your Ninja Foodi. Begin by removing all packaging materials and washing the baskets and crisper plates with warm, soapy water. This will ensure that your first meal isn't tainted by any residual manufacturing materials. Dry everything thoroughly before reassembling the unit.

Next, place your Ninja Foodi on a flat, stable surface in your kitchen. Make sure it's positioned with plenty of space around it for proper ventilation—this is especially important because the air fryer uses high heat and needs to disperse it safely. Plug in the unit, and you're ready to explore the exciting features of your new kitchen companion.

Understanding the Functions: Air Fry, Roast, Bake, and More

The Ninja Foodi 2-Basket Air Fryer is more than just an air fryer—it's a multi-functional powerhouse that can replace several other kitchen gadgets. Understanding its different functions will help you make the most out of your new appliance.

1. **Air Fry**: This is the most popular function and for good reason. The Air Fry setting circulates hot air around the food, giving it a crispy texture similar to deep frying but with significantly less oil. Use this setting for anything from French fries to chicken wings to vegetables.

2. **Air Roast**: This function is perfect for roasting meats and vegetables. It uses a combination of high heat and convection to cook food evenly, producing a tender inside and a crispy outside. Think of it as your go-to for Sunday roasts or perfectly caramelized root vegetables.

3. **Air Broil**: For those times when you need a high-heat sear or a crispy finish on the top of your dish, the Air Broil function is ideal. Use it for melting cheese on a casserole, crisping up the skin on chicken, or finishing a dish with a golden-brown crust.

4. **Bake**: The Bake function turns your air fryer into a mini oven, allowing you to bake everything from cakes to bread to casseroles. It provides even heat distribution, making it easier to bake goods without having to heat up your entire kitchen with a conventional oven.

5. **Reheat**: Say goodbye to soggy leftovers. The Reheat function brings back the freshness to your previously cooked meals by using hot air to revive their crispy texture and warmth without overcooking them.

6. **Dehydrate**: For those who love healthy snacks, the Dehydrate function allows you to make your own dried fruits, vegetables, and even jerky. It operates at a low temperature to remove moisture from foods while preserving their nutrients.

By understanding these functions, you can begin to see how the Ninja Foodi 2-Basket Air Fryer can streamline your cooking process. Whether you're preparing a quick weeknight dinner or experimenting with a new recipe, this appliance is designed to adapt to your culinary needs.

Exploring the DualZone Technology: How to Cook Two Foods at Once

One of the most exciting features of the Ninja Foodi 2-Basket Air Fryer is its DualZone technology, which allows you to cook two different foods at once using separate temperature and time settings. This innovation is a true game-changer, especially for busy households where different dietary preferences or timing constraints can make meal preparation a challenge.

The key to mastering DualZone technology is understanding the two main settings: **SyncCook** and **SyncFinish**.

- **SyncCook**: This setting allows both baskets to cook the same food at the same temperature and time. It's perfect for when you're making a large batch of the same dish, like fries or chicken nuggets, and need extra capacity.

Simply select the SyncCook option, set your desired temperature and time, and the Ninja Foodi will ensure both baskets are cooking in unison.

- **SyncFinish**: This setting is where DualZone technology truly shines. SyncFinish lets you cook two different foods that have different cooking times and temperatures, but ensures they finish at the same time. For example, you can cook a piece of fish at 400°F (200°C) in one basket while roasting potatoes at 350°F (175°C) in the other. The Ninja Foodi automatically adjusts the cooking times so that both dishes are ready to serve simultaneously.

To use SyncFinish, simply select the function, temperature, and time for the first basket, then repeat the process for the second basket. Press the start button, and the air fryer will take care of the rest. This feature not only saves you time but also simplifies meal prep, allowing you to focus on other tasks while the Ninja Foodi works its magic.

DualZone technology also encourages creativity in the kitchen. You can pair different foods together to create balanced meals, experiment with new flavor combinations, or even cook a main dish and a side dish simultaneously. The possibilities are endless, and as you become more comfortable with your Ninja Foodi, you'll find yourself experimenting with new recipes and techniques that make meal preparation both fun and efficient.

Care and Maintenance: Keeping Your Air Fryer in Top Condition

Like any kitchen appliance, your Ninja Foodi 2-Basket Air Fryer will perform best and last longer with proper care and maintenance. Fortunately, the Ninja Foodi is designed to be easy to clean and maintain, so you can spend more time enjoying your meals and less time worrying about upkeep.

Here are some simple tips to keep your air fryer in top condition:

1. **Clean After Each Use**: After every cooking session, make sure to clean the baskets, crisper plates, and any other removable parts with warm, soapy water. This prevents food residue from building up and ensures that your air fryer is ready for its next use. For stubborn residue, soak the parts in warm water for a few minutes before scrubbing gently with a non-abrasive sponge.

2. **Wipe Down the Interior and Exterior**: Occasionally, food particles or grease may splatter inside the air fryer. Use a damp cloth to wipe down the interior walls and the heating element. Be sure to unplug the unit and allow it to cool completely before cleaning. For the exterior, a quick wipe with a damp cloth will keep it looking new.

3. **Avoid Abrasive Cleaners**: To protect the non-stick coating on the baskets and crisper plates, avoid using abrasive cleaners, metal utensils, or scouring pads. Stick to soft sponges or cloths and mild dish soap.

4. **Check the Air Intake and Exhaust**: The Ninja Foodi relies on proper airflow to function effectively. Periodically check the air intake and exhaust vents to ensure they are clear of dust and debris. This will help maintain optimal performance and prevent overheating.

5. **Descale the Heating Element**: If you notice any discoloration or build-up on the heating element, it may be time to descale. You can do this by wiping the element with a mixture of vinegar and water, then rinsing with a damp cloth. Always ensure the element is completely dry before using the air fryer again.

By following these simple maintenance tips, you'll keep your Ninja Foodi 2-Basket Air Fryer performing at its best for years to come.

Troubleshooting Common Issues

Even with the best care, you may occasionally encounter some issues with your air fryer. Here are a few common problems and how to solve them:

1. **Uneven Cooking**: If your food is cooking unevenly, it may be due to overcrowding in the baskets or uneven food placement. Try reducing the amount of food in the basket or shaking the basket halfway through cooking to redistribute the food.

2. **Food Sticking to the Basket**: If food is sticking to the basket, ensure that you're using enough oil or cooking spray to lightly coat the food. Also, make sure the basket is clean and dry before adding food.

3. **The Air Fryer Isn't Turning On**: If your Ninja Foodi isn't powering on, check that it's properly plugged into an outlet and that the outlet is functioning. Also, ensure that the baskets are fully inserted and the unit is closed correctly, as the air fryer will not operate if these components are not securely in place.

4. **The Air Fryer Stops Mid-Cooking**: If your air fryer stops cooking unexpectedly, it could be due to overheating. Allow the unit to cool down for a few minutes before restarting. Ensure that there is enough space around the unit for proper ventilation.

5. **Strange Smells or Smoke**: If you notice an unusual smell or see smoke coming from your air fryer, it may be due to food particles or grease trapped in the heating element. Turn off the unit, unplug it, and allow it to cool before cleaning the interior thoroughly.

By troubleshooting these common issues, you can quickly resolve any problems and get back to enjoying your cooking experience with the Ninja Foodi 2-Basket Air Fryer.

As you become more familiar with your Ninja Foodi, you'll discover just how versatile and user-friendly it is. This chapter has provided you with the foundational knowledge you need to get started, from unboxing and setting up your air fryer to understanding its functions and troubleshooting any issues. Now that you're equipped with the basics, you're ready to dive into the delicious world of air frying with confidence and ease.

Chapter 2: Air Fryer Fundamentals

How Air Frying Works: The Science Behind the Crisp

Air frying has quickly become one of the most popular cooking methods in modern kitchens, and it's easy to see why. It promises the delicious, crispy texture of fried foods without the need for excessive oil, making it a healthier alternative to traditional frying. But how exactly does air frying work? Understanding the science behind the crisp will not only deepen your appreciation for this versatile cooking method but also help you achieve perfect results every time you use your Ninja Foodi 2-Basket Air Fryer.

At its core, air frying is a method of cooking that uses hot air circulation to cook food evenly and create a crispy exterior. The Ninja Foodi 2-Basket Air Fryer is equipped with powerful heating elements and high-speed fans that work together to circulate hot air around the food. This rapid air circulation, combined with a small amount of oil (or none at all), creates a Maillard reaction—a chemical reaction between amino acids and reducing sugars that gives browned food its distinctive flavor and texture.

The Ninja Foodi's design ensures that the hot air reaches every part of the food, which is why you get that desirable crispy finish on all sides, not just the top. Unlike traditional frying, which requires submerging food in oil, air frying cooks food from the outside in, allowing the exterior to crisp up while the interior remains tender and juicy.

One of the key benefits of air frying is that it allows you to achieve the same results as deep frying but with significantly less oil—sometimes up to 75% less. This means you can enjoy your favorite fried foods, like French fries, chicken wings, and onion rings, with fewer calories and less fat. Plus, because air frying cooks food quickly and evenly, it often results in less oil absorption, making the food lighter and less greasy.

Another advantage of air frying is its versatility. While it's excellent for achieving that crispy texture we all love, it's also great for roasting, baking, and even dehydrating. The same principles of hot air circulation apply, making it a go-to appliance for a wide variety of dishes. Whether you're air frying, roasting, or baking, the Ninja Foodi 2-Basket Air Fryer offers a healthier way to cook your favorite meals without compromising on taste or texture.

Best Practices for Perfectly Cooked Meals Every Time

To get the most out of your Ninja Foodi 2-Basket Air Fryer and ensure your meals come out perfectly every time, there are a few best practices to keep in mind. These tips will help you avoid common mistakes and maximize the potential of your air fryer.

1. **Preheat Your Air Fryer**: While the Ninja Foodi heats up quickly, preheating can make a big difference, especially for recipes that require a crispy exterior. Preheating ensures that the air fryer is at the right temperature before you start cooking, which helps food cook more evenly and reduces cooking time. Most recipes will indicate whether preheating is necessary, so be sure to follow those guidelines.

2. **Don't Overcrowd the Baskets**: For the best results, avoid overcrowding the baskets. When food is packed too tightly, the hot air can't circulate properly, which can lead to uneven cooking and less crispy results. If you're cooking a large quantity of food, consider cooking in batches to ensure that each piece gets enough exposure to the hot air.

3. **Shake or Flip Halfway Through**: To promote even cooking, especially for smaller items like fries or chicken nuggets, it's a good idea to shake the basket or flip the food halfway through the cooking time. This helps redistribute the food, ensuring that all sides get crispy and golden. The Ninja Foodi will pause cooking when you open the baskets, allowing you to check on your food and make adjustments as needed.

4. **Use a Light Coat of Oil**: While one of the benefits of air frying is that it requires little to no oil, a light coat of oil can help enhance the crispiness of certain foods. Use a high smoke point oil, like avocado oil or olive oil, and apply it with a spray bottle or brush to avoid overdoing it. Remember, a little goes a long way in the air fryer.

5. **Choose the Right Temperature**: Different foods require different cooking temperatures to achieve the best results. Higher temperatures are great for creating a crispy exterior, while lower temperatures are better for cooking food through without burning it. Be sure to follow the temperature guidelines provided in the recipes and adjust based on your preferences and experience.

6. **Monitor Cooking Progress**: While the Ninja Foodi is designed to cook food quickly and evenly, it's always a good idea to check on your food periodically, especially when you're trying a new recipe. This allows you to make any necessary adjustments to cooking time or temperature and ensures that your meal comes out exactly the way you want it.

7. **Rest Before Serving**: Just like with other cooking methods, letting food rest for a few minutes after air frying can help it retain its juices and enhance the overall flavor. This is especially important for meats, which can dry out if sliced immediately after cooking.

By incorporating these best practices into your air frying routine, you'll be well on your way to consistently delicious meals with your Ninja Foodi 2-Basket Air Fryer.

Essential Tools and Accessories for Your Ninja Foodi

To truly maximize the potential of your Ninja Foodi 2-Basket Air Fryer, there are a few essential tools and accessories that can make your cooking experience even more efficient and enjoyable. While the appliance itself is quite versatile, these additional items can help you expand your culinary repertoire and achieve even better results.

1. **Oil Spray Bottle**: As mentioned earlier, a light coat of oil can help enhance the crispiness of your food. An oil spray bottle allows you to evenly distribute a small amount of oil without overdoing it. Look for a bottle that is easy to refill and produces a fine mist for the best results.

2. **Silicone Tongs**: Silicone tongs are perfect for flipping and removing food from the air fryer baskets without scratching the non-stick coating. They're also heat-resistant, making them safe to use with the high temperatures of the air fryer.

3. **Perforated Parchment Paper**: Perforated parchment paper is a great accessory for preventing food from sticking to the crisper plates while still allowing air to circulate. The perforations ensure that the hot air reaches all sides of the food, helping it cook evenly and preventing sogginess.

4. **Cooking Thermometer**: For meats and other temperature-sensitive foods, a cooking thermometer is an invaluable tool. It helps you ensure that your food is cooked to the appropriate internal temperature, which is especially important for safety and achieving the desired doneness.

5. **Baking Dishes and Molds**: If you enjoy baking, consider investing in air fryer-safe baking dishes and molds. These allow you to expand your air fryer's capabilities beyond frying and roasting. From muffins to casseroles, having the right bakeware can make all the difference.

6. **Silicone Basting Brush**: A silicone basting brush is perfect for applying marinades, sauces, or oil to your food without making a mess. It's easy to clean and won't absorb flavors, making it ideal for multiple uses.

7. **Food Divider**: A food divider can be useful when cooking multiple items in the same basket, keeping them separate and preventing flavors from mingling. This is especially handy if you're cooking for people with different dietary preferences or restrictions.

8. **Non-Stick Baking Mats**: Non-stick baking mats are another great accessory for preventing sticking and making cleanup easier. They're reusable, easy to clean, and help ensure that your food cooks evenly without sticking to the baskets.

Having these tools and accessories on hand will enhance your Ninja Foodi experience, making it easier to prepare a wider variety of dishes with minimal hassle.

Ingredient Preparation Tips for Consistent Results

To achieve consistent and delicious results with your Ninja Foodi 2-Basket Air Fryer, it's important to pay attention to how you prepare your ingredients. Proper preparation can make the difference between a perfectly cooked dish and one that falls short of your expectations.

1. **Cut Ingredients Uniformly**: One of the keys to even cooking is to cut your ingredients into uniform pieces. Whether you're chopping vegetables, slicing potatoes, or portioning out meat, make sure the pieces are roughly the same size. This ensures that everything cooks at the same rate, preventing some pieces from being overcooked while others are undercooked.

2. **Pat Ingredients Dry**: Moisture is the enemy of crispiness. Before air frying, be sure to pat your ingredients dry with a paper towel, especially if you're cooking something like potatoes, chicken, or fish. Removing excess moisture allows the food to crisp up more effectively and prevents it from steaming instead of frying.

3. **Season Generously**: Don't be afraid to season your food generously before air frying. The hot air circulation in the air fryer can sometimes cause seasonings to lose potency, so it's a good idea to add a little extra salt, pepper, or your favorite spices. You can also marinate your ingredients ahead of time to infuse them with even more flavor.

4. **Toss with Oil or Sauce**: If your recipe calls for it, toss your ingredients with a small amount of oil or sauce before placing them in the air fryer. This helps the food crisp up and caramelize while cooking. Just remember to use oil sparingly to avoid excess grease.

5. **Arrange Food in a Single Layer**: For the best results, arrange your food in a single layer in the air fryer baskets. This ensures that the hot air can circulate around each piece, cooking it evenly on all sides. If you're cooking a larger quantity, consider doing it in batches rather than overcrowding the baskets.

6. **Preheat Ingredients**: For some recipes, especially those involving frozen foods, it's helpful to let the ingredients sit at room temperature for a few minutes before cooking. This reduces the cooking time and helps the food cook more evenly. However, be mindful of food safety guidelines, particularly with raw meats.

7. **Use a Light Coating**: For breaded items, such as chicken tenders or fish fillets, a light coating of breadcrumbs or panko can enhance the crispiness. Just be sure to press the coating firmly onto the food so that it adheres well during cooking.

By following these preparation tips, you'll set yourself up for success with every meal you prepare in your Ninja Foodi 2-Basket Air Fryer.

How to Convert Your Favorite Recipes for the Air Fryer

One of the best things about owning a Ninja Foodi 2-Basket Air Fryer is that you can easily adapt many of your favorite recipes for this versatile appliance. With a few simple adjustments, you can enjoy healthier versions of your go-to dishes, all with that signature crispy texture that air frying provides.

1. **Adjust the Temperature**: When converting recipes for the air fryer, a general rule of thumb is to reduce the cooking temperature by about 25°F (15°C) compared to traditional oven baking. This is because the air fryer's convection heat is more efficient at cooking food quickly and evenly.

2. **Reduce the Cooking Time**: Since the air fryer cooks food faster than traditional methods, you'll also need to reduce the cooking time. Start by reducing the time by about 20% and then check the food periodically. You can always add more time if needed, but it's harder to salvage food that's been overcooked.

3. **Monitor Closely**: The first time you convert a recipe for the air fryer, it's important to monitor the cooking process closely. Check on the food frequently to ensure it's cooking as expected and make adjustments as necessary. Once you've perfected the timing and temperature, you can confidently replicate the recipe in the future.

4. **Consider the Cooking Method**: Some recipes are naturally suited to air frying, such as those that involve frying, roasting, or baking. Others may require more creativity. For example, if a recipe calls for grilling, you can use the air fryer's broil function to achieve similar results. If it's a stovetop recipe, you may need to experiment with the air fryer's settings to find the best approach.

5. **Use the Right Cookware**: If your original recipe requires a specific type of cookware, such as a baking dish or muffin tin, make sure it's compatible with the air fryer. Silicone molds, mini baking pans, and air fryer-safe dishes are great options for adapting recipes that require specific shapes or structures.

6. **Test and Tweak**: Converting recipes for the air fryer can be a bit of a trial-and-error process, especially if the original recipe wasn't designed with this appliance in mind. Don't be discouraged if your first attempt doesn't turn out perfectly—use it as an opportunity to tweak and improve the recipe for next time.

By learning how to convert your favorite recipes for the air fryer, you can enjoy a wide variety of dishes that are healthier and quicker to prepare. Whether you're making a classic comfort food or experimenting with a new cuisine, the Ninja Foodi 2-Basket Air Fryer is a powerful tool that makes it easy to create delicious, nutritious meals with minimal effort.

Chapter 3: Maximizing Efficiency with Dual Baskets

Sync and Match: Understanding the DualZone Settings

The Ninja Foodi 2-Basket Air Fryer's DualZone technology is truly a game-changer in the kitchen, especially when it comes to multitasking and saving time. Understanding how to use the Sync and Match settings will allow you to make the most of this feature, transforming how you approach meal preparation.

SyncCook and **SyncFinish** are the two primary functions that make DualZone technology so versatile. Let's break down each of these settings so you can start using them with confidence.

SyncCook is perfect for when you want to cook a large batch of the same food item. Suppose you're preparing a big batch of French fries or chicken wings for a family gathering. With SyncCook, both baskets will cook the same food at the same temperature and for the same amount of time. This means you can double your output without compromising on the quality or consistency of the results. Simply set the temperature and time for one basket, press the SyncCook button, and the Ninja Foodi will automatically apply the same settings to the second basket.

On the other hand, **SyncFinish** is where the magic of multitasking happens. This setting allows you to cook two completely different foods with different cooking times and temperatures, but ensures that they finish cooking at the same time. Imagine cooking a protein, like salmon, in one basket while roasting vegetables in the other. With SyncFinish, you can set the optimal time and temperature for each basket individually, and the Ninja Foodi will coordinate the cooking so that everything is ready to serve together. It's a seamless way to prepare balanced meals without having to juggle multiple timers or worry about one dish getting cold while you finish the other.

To use SyncFinish, start by selecting the cooking function, temperature, and time for the first basket. Once you've done that, move on to the second basket and set the desired cooking parameters. Press the SyncFinish button, and your Ninja

Foodi will take care of the rest. This feature is particularly useful for busy weeknights when you want to get dinner on the table quickly without sacrificing variety or quality.

Understanding these DualZone settings is key to maximizing the efficiency of your Ninja Foodi 2-Basket Air Fryer. Whether you're cooking for a crowd or just trying to simplify your daily meal prep, these features allow you to do more in less time.

Cooking Two Dishes at Once: Pairing Ideas for Balanced Meals

One of the most exciting aspects of the DualZone technology is the ability to cook two different dishes simultaneously. This not only saves time but also makes it easier to create balanced, nutritious meals that everyone in the family will love. The key to successfully cooking two dishes at once is to choose foods that complement each other in terms of cooking time and temperature.

Here are some pairing ideas to get you started:

1. **Chicken and Vegetables**: Pair chicken breasts or thighs with a medley of vegetables like carrots, zucchini, and bell peppers. Set one basket to air fry the chicken at 375°F (190°C) for about 20 minutes, and the other basket to roast the vegetables at 350°F (175°C) for the same amount of time using the SyncFinish feature. The result is a complete, well-balanced meal with minimal effort.

2. **Salmon and Asparagus**: Salmon fillets and asparagus spears make a perfect duo. Cook the salmon in one basket at 400°F (200°C) for 12 minutes and the asparagus in the other basket at 375°F (190°C) for 10 minutes. Use SyncFinish to ensure both are ready at the same time, leaving you with a restaurant-quality dinner.

3. **Pork Chops and Sweet Potatoes**: For a hearty meal, pair air-fried pork chops with roasted sweet potato wedges. The pork chops can be cooked at 375°F (190°C) for 15 minutes, while the sweet potatoes roast at 350°F (175°C) for 25 minutes. SyncFinish will coordinate the timing so everything comes out hot and ready to serve together.

4. **Shrimp and Brussels Sprouts**: This combination is both flavorful and quick. Cook the shrimp in one basket at 400°F (200°C) for 8 minutes, and the Brussels sprouts in the other basket at 375°F (190°C) for 15 minutes. With SyncFinish, you'll have a delicious meal that's ready to plate in no time.

5. **Tofu and Broccoli**: For a plant-based option, pair crispy tofu with roasted broccoli. The tofu can be air-fried at 375°F (190°C) for 20 minutes, while the broccoli roasts at 350°F (175°C) for 18 minutes. SyncFinish ensures both components are perfectly cooked and ready to enjoy together.

When pairing dishes, it's important to consider the cooking methods and how they complement each other. For example, roasting vegetables and air frying proteins at the same time can create a balanced meal with varied textures and flavors. Experiment with different combinations to discover your favorite pairings, and remember that the Ninja Foodi 2-Basket Air Fryer is designed to handle the heavy lifting, allowing you to focus on enjoying your meal.

Tips for Timing and Temperature Coordination

Coordinating timing and temperature is essential for getting the best results when using the DualZone feature. Here are some practical tips to help you master this aspect of air frying:

1. **Start with Similar Cooking Times**: When first experimenting with DualZone cooking, it's easiest to pair foods that have similar cooking times. This minimizes the need for complex timing adjustments and allows you to get comfortable with the SyncFinish feature.

2. **Adjust as Needed**: If one food finishes before the other, don't worry! The Ninja Foodi 2-Basket Air Fryer allows you to pause cooking in one basket while the other continues. This feature is particularly useful if you're working with foods that have a more significant difference in cooking times.

3. **Stagger Start Times**: If you're not using SyncFinish, you can manually stagger the start times of each basket to ensure that both foods are ready at the same time. For example, if you're cooking something that takes 20 minutes in one basket and 15 minutes in the other, start the longer-cooking food first, then add the second food five minutes later.

4. **Use the Right Temperature for Each Food**: Don't be afraid to use different temperatures for each basket, as this is one of the main advantages of the DualZone technology. Higher temperatures are great for creating a crispy exterior, while lower temperatures are better for roasting or baking. The Ninja Foodi's design ensures that both baskets maintain their set temperatures, so you can cook each food to perfection.

5. **Check on Your Food**: While the Ninja Foodi is designed to cook food evenly, it's still a good idea to check on your food periodically, especially when you're cooking two different dishes at once. This allows you to make any necessary adjustments and ensures that nothing overcooks.

6. **Plan for Resting Time**: Some foods, particularly meats, benefit from a few minutes of resting time after cooking. Factor this into your timing to ensure everything is ready to serve at the same time.

With these tips, you'll be able to coordinate timing and temperature effectively, making it easy to prepare complex meals with multiple components.

Quick and Easy Meal Planning with Dual Baskets

The Ninja Foodi 2-Basket Air Fryer's DualZone technology is a powerful tool for meal planning, especially for busy individuals and families. By planning your meals with the Dual Baskets in mind, you can streamline your cooking process and ensure that you're always ready to serve a delicious, well-balanced meal.

Here are some strategies for quick and easy meal planning:

1. **Batch Cooking**: Use the Dual Baskets to batch cook components of your meals. For example, you can cook a large batch of roasted vegetables in one basket while air frying chicken breasts in the other. Store the cooked components in the fridge or freezer, and mix and match them throughout the week for quick, healthy meals.

2. **Theme Nights**: Plan theme nights where you cook two complementary dishes that fit a specific cuisine or dietary preference. For example, you might have a Mediterranean night with air-fried falafel and roasted vegetables, or a Tex-Mex night with air-fried chicken fajitas and crispy tortilla chips.

3. **Prep Ahead**: Prep your ingredients ahead of time so that they're ready to go when you're ready to cook. Chop vegetables, marinate proteins, and portion out seasonings in advance. When it's time to cook, simply load the baskets and set the DualZone settings for a quick, hassle-free meal.

4. **Use Leftovers Creatively**: If you have leftovers, use the Dual Baskets to reheat them while cooking a new dish. For example, reheat yesterday's roasted vegetables in one basket while air frying fresh chicken tenders in the other. This not only reduces food waste but also saves you time.

5. **Plan for Versatility**: Choose recipes that are versatile and can be paired with a variety of sides or mains. For example, air-fried tofu can be paired with different vegetables, grains, or sauces throughout the week, giving you flexibility in your meal planning.

By incorporating these strategies into your meal planning routine, you can make the most of your Ninja Foodi 2-Basket Air Fryer and enjoy delicious, home-cooked meals with minimal effort.

Creative Uses for the Dual Baskets: Beyond Dinner

While the Ninja Foodi 2-Basket Air Fryer is fantastic for preparing dinner, its versatility extends far beyond the evening meal. Here are some creative ways to use the Dual Baskets for breakfast, lunch, snacks, and even desserts:

1. **Breakfast Combos**: Use one basket to air fry breakfast potatoes or hash browns while cooking bacon or sausage in the other. You can also prepare a batch of air-fried eggs in one basket and toast in the other for a complete breakfast.

2. **Lunch Prep**: For a quick and easy lunch, use one basket to air fry a protein like chicken breast or tofu while roasting vegetables in the other. You can then use these components to assemble salads, grain bowls, or wraps throughout the week.

3. **Snack Time**: Air fry a batch of sweet potato fries or zucchini chips in one basket while roasting nuts or making air-popped popcorn in the other. This allows you to prepare a variety of healthy snacks that are perfect for munching throughout the day.

4. **Dessert Pairings**: Yes, you can even use the Dual Baskets for dessert! Air fry apple slices with cinnamon sugar in one basket while baking oatmeal cookies in the other. The combination of warm apples and freshly baked cookies is sure to satisfy any sweet tooth.

5. **Meal Prep for the Week**: Use the Dual Baskets to prep multiple meal components at once, such as roasted vegetables in one basket and grilled chicken in the other. Store the cooked components in the fridge, and mix and match them throughout the week for quick, healthy meals.

6. **Holiday Cooking**: During the holidays, the Dual Baskets can be a lifesaver when you need to cook multiple dishes at once. Use one basket to air fry a batch of appetizers, like stuffed mushrooms or bacon-wrapped dates, while cooking a side dish in the other.

By thinking creatively and exploring the full potential of the Dual Baskets, you can expand your culinary horizons and make the Ninja Foodi 2-Basket Air Fryer an indispensable tool in your kitchen. Whether you're preparing meals for a busy weeknight, hosting a dinner party, or simply trying out new recipes, the Dual Baskets offer endless possibilities for delicious, convenient cooking.

Chapter 4: Healthy Cooking with Your Air Fryer

Reducing Fat and Calories Without Losing Flavor

One of the most appealing benefits of using the Ninja Foodi 2-Basket Air Fryer is the ability to create delicious, crispy dishes with significantly less fat and calories than traditional frying methods. The air fryer uses hot air circulation to achieve that coveted crispy texture, meaning you can enjoy your favorite fried foods without the excess oil. But how can you ensure that your meals are both flavorful and health-conscious? Let's explore some strategies.

First, it's important to understand that fat can be an important flavor carrier in cooking. However, with the Ninja Foodi, you can reduce the amount of oil you use without sacrificing taste. A light mist of oil sprayed directly onto your food is often all you need to achieve a crispy, golden finish. This minimal amount of oil adds flavor and helps with browning, but without the heavy calorie load of deep frying.

Additionally, you can enhance the flavor of your dishes by incorporating herbs, spices, and aromatics. For example, instead of relying on fat to bring richness to a dish, consider seasoning your food with garlic, onion powder, paprika, or fresh herbs like rosemary and thyme. These ingredients add depth and complexity to your meals, making them both healthier and more satisfying.

Another technique is to use acidic ingredients like lemon juice, vinegar, or mustard, which can brighten up flavors and make dishes taste more vibrant. These ingredients are especially effective in marinades or as finishing touches on cooked dishes. For instance, a squeeze of lemon over air-fried fish can elevate the flavors without adding unnecessary fat.

Lastly, consider substituting high-fat ingredients with lower-fat alternatives. For example, use Greek yogurt instead of sour cream, or swap mayonnaise for a lighter option like mashed avocado or hummus. These swaps can reduce the overall calorie content of your meals while still providing a creamy, satisfying texture.

Understanding Nutritional Labels: Making Healthier Choices

When it comes to healthy cooking, understanding nutritional labels is crucial. Being able to read and interpret these labels allows you to make informed decisions about the ingredients you use in your Ninja Foodi 2-Basket Air Fryer. Here's a step-by-step guide to help you decode the most important information on food labels.

1. **Serving Size**: Always start by checking the serving size at the top of the label. This tells you the portion of food that the nutritional information applies to. Be aware that many packages contain multiple servings, so if you eat more than the serving size listed, you'll need to adjust the nutritional information accordingly.

2. **Calories**: The calorie count gives you an idea of how much energy you'll get from a serving of the food. While it's not necessary to count every calorie, it's helpful to have a general idea of how calorie-dense certain foods are, especially if you're trying to manage your weight or reduce your calorie intake.

3. **Total Fat**: This section shows the total amount of fat per serving, broken down into saturated fat, trans fat, and sometimes polyunsaturated and monounsaturated fats. Aim to choose foods that are lower in saturated and trans fats, as these can contribute to heart disease. The Ninja Foodi helps by allowing you to cook with less added fat, but it's still important to monitor the fat content of the foods you're air frying.

4. **Cholesterol and Sodium**: These nutrients are important to monitor, particularly if you have heart concerns or high blood pressure. Many processed foods are high in sodium, so using your air fryer to prepare fresh, whole foods can help you control your intake.

5. **Total Carbohydrates**: This section includes fiber, sugars, and sometimes added sugars. Aim for foods higher in fiber and lower in added sugars. Fiber helps with digestion and can keep you feeling fuller longer, which is beneficial for weight management.

6. **Protein**: Protein is essential for building and repairing tissues, and it also helps keep you satisfied. Look for ingredients that provide a good source of protein, especially if you're following a specific dietary plan like keto or low-carb.

7. **Vitamins and Minerals**: Nutritional labels also list the percentage of daily values for important vitamins and minerals, such as vitamin D, calcium, iron, and potassium. Choose foods that contribute to your daily nutrient needs, especially if you have specific dietary requirements.

By understanding these key components of nutritional labels, you can make healthier choices when selecting ingredients for your air fryer recipes. This knowledge empowers you to create meals that are not only delicious but also aligned with your health goals.

Tips for Cooking with Less Oil

One of the Ninja Foodi 2-Basket Air Fryer's greatest advantages is its ability to cook with very little oil while still producing crisp, flavorful results. Here are some tips for making the most of this feature:

1. **Use a High-Quality Oil Spray**: Investing in a good oil spray bottle allows you to control the amount of oil you're using. A quick, even mist of oil over your food is usually enough to enhance crispiness without adding too many extra calories. Choose oils with a high smoke point, like avocado oil or extra light olive oil, which are ideal for air frying.

2. **Apply Oil Directly to the Food**: Instead of adding oil to the basket, apply it directly to the food. This not only reduces the amount of oil needed but also ensures that it's distributed evenly, helping your food to brown and crisp up nicely.

3. **Experiment with Oil-Free Cooking**: Many foods, especially those with natural moisture content, can be air-fried without any oil at all. Vegetables like zucchini, bell peppers, and mushrooms often don't need added oil to achieve a delicious, roasted flavor. For protein, try air frying skin-on chicken or fatty fish like salmon, which release natural oils during cooking.

4. **Use Alternative Cooking Methods**: Consider steaming or parboiling vegetables before air frying them. This pre-cooking method reduces the amount of oil needed to achieve a tender-crisp texture. It also speeds up the air frying process, making meal prep even quicker.

5. **Opt for Lean Cuts of Meat**: When air frying meats, choose lean cuts like chicken breast or pork tenderloin. These cuts require less oil to cook through and stay moist. If you prefer using skin-on or fattier cuts, like chicken thighs, the Ninja Foodi will allow the natural fats to render out, reducing the need for added oil.

By incorporating these tips, you'll be able to cook healthier meals that are lower in fat but still full of flavor. The Ninja Foodi's ability to use less oil without sacrificing taste makes it a powerful tool for anyone looking to improve their diet.

Incorporating More Vegetables into Your Meals

Vegetables are an essential part of a healthy diet, providing essential vitamins, minerals, and fiber. The Ninja Foodi 2-Basket Air Fryer makes it easier than ever to incorporate more vegetables into your meals, thanks to its ability to roast, crisp, and even dehydrate a wide variety of produce.

Here are some ideas for adding more vegetables to your diet using the air fryer:

1. **Roasted Vegetables**: Roasting vegetables in the air fryer is quick and easy. Simply chop your vegetables into uniform pieces, toss them with a little oil and seasoning, and air fry them at 375°F (190°C) until they're tender and slightly caramelized. Vegetables like Brussels sprouts, sweet potatoes, carrots, and broccoli are perfect for this method.

2. **Vegetable Chips**: Make your own vegetable chips for a healthy, crunchy snack. Slice vegetables like zucchini, beets, or kale thinly, season them lightly, and air fry until crisp. These chips are a great alternative to store-bought options and can be enjoyed on their own or with a healthy dip.

3. **Stuffed Vegetables**: Use the air fryer to prepare stuffed vegetables like bell peppers or zucchini boats. Fill them with a mixture of lean protein, grains, and cheese, and air fry until the vegetables are tender and the filling is heated through.

4. **Vegetable Skewers**: Thread your favorite vegetables onto skewers, brush them with a little oil and seasoning, and air fry for a quick and flavorful side dish. This is a great way to prepare a variety of vegetables at once and adds a fun presentation to your meals.

5. **Adding Vegetables to Main Dishes**: Incorporate vegetables into your main dishes by air frying them alongside your protein. For example, cook chicken and vegetables together in the dual baskets, or add chopped vegetables to casseroles and bakes prepared in the air fryer. This method not only increases your vegetable intake but also adds color and texture to your meals.

By making vegetables a central part of your cooking routine, you'll naturally increase your intake of these nutrient-rich foods. The Ninja Foodi 2-Basket Air Fryer makes it easy and convenient to prepare a variety of vegetables, ensuring that you never get bored with your options.

Adapting to Dietary Restrictions: Gluten-Free, Keto, and More

The Ninja Foodi 2-Basket Air Fryer is incredibly versatile, making it easy to adapt your cooking to a wide range of dietary restrictions and preferences. Whether you're following a gluten-free, keto, vegetarian, or other specialized diet, this appliance can help you create delicious meals that meet your needs.

1. **Gluten-Free Cooking**: The air fryer is perfect for preparing gluten-free meals, as it allows you to create crispy, breaded dishes without the need for traditional flour-based coatings. Use almond flour, coconut flour, or gluten-free breadcrumbs to coat proteins like chicken or fish. Additionally, you can air fry gluten-free snacks like sweet potato fries or roasted chickpeas for a healthy, satisfying treat.

2. **Keto and Low-Carb Diets**: If you're following a keto or low-carb diet, the air fryer is a great tool for preparing meals that are high in healthy fats and low in carbohydrates. Use it to cook keto-friendly proteins like salmon, bacon, or eggs, and pair them with low-carb vegetables like cauliflower, zucchini, and spinach. You can also make keto-friendly snacks like cheese crisps or avocado fries in the air fryer.

3. **Vegetarian and Vegan Diets**: The Ninja Foodi is also ideal for preparing plant-based meals. Air fry tofu, tempeh, or chickpeas for a protein-packed addition to salads and grain bowls. You can also use the air fryer to prepare veggie burgers, falafel, or roasted vegetables for a hearty and satisfying meal.

4. **Dairy-Free Cooking**: For those who are dairy-free, the air fryer allows you to create creamy, flavorful dishes without relying on dairy products. Use plant-based oils, dairy-free cheeses, and alternative milks to prepare your favorite recipes. The air fryer is also perfect for making dairy-free desserts like baked apples or coconut macaroons.

5. **Adapting Recipes**: Many traditional recipes can be easily adapted to suit your dietary needs when using the air fryer. Simply swap out ingredients to fit your diet, such as using gluten-free flour for breading or replacing high-carb vegetables with lower-carb options. The Ninja Foodi's versatility makes it easy to experiment with different ingredients and find what works best for you.

By understanding how to adapt your cooking to meet specific dietary restrictions, you can enjoy a wide variety of healthy, delicious meals without feeling limited. The Ninja Foodi 2-Basket Air Fryer is a powerful tool that supports a range of dietary needs, making it easier than ever to cook in a way that's aligned with your health goals.

Chapter 5: Troubleshooting and FAQs

Avoiding Common Mistakes: What Not to Do

Even though the Ninja Foodi 2-Basket Air Fryer is designed to be user-friendly, it's still possible to make a few missteps along the way, especially if you're new to air frying. Understanding these common mistakes and how to avoid them will help you get the most out of your appliance and ensure that your meals turn out perfectly every time.

1. Overcrowding the Baskets: One of the most common mistakes when using an air fryer is overcrowding the baskets. When you pile too much food into the baskets, the hot air can't circulate properly, leading to uneven cooking and less crispy results. To avoid this, always arrange your food in a single layer with some space between pieces. If you're cooking for a crowd, consider cooking in batches to ensure that each piece gets that perfect golden-brown finish.

2. Skipping the Preheat: While the Ninja Foodi heats up quickly, skipping the preheat step can affect the cooking time and the texture of your food. Preheating ensures that the air fryer reaches the desired temperature before you start cooking, which is particularly important for recipes that require a crispy exterior. Always check the recipe to see if preheating is recommended and follow those instructions for the best results.

3. Using Too Much Oil: One of the benefits of air frying is that it requires far less oil than traditional frying methods. However, using too much oil can lead to soggy results and excess smoke during cooking. A light mist of oil is usually all you need. Use a spray bottle to apply the oil evenly over your food rather than drizzling or pouring it directly.

4. Neglecting to Shake or Flip: For foods like fries, nuggets, or any small items that need even browning, it's important to shake the basket or flip the food halfway through cooking. This ensures that all sides are exposed to the hot air, resulting in an evenly cooked dish. The Ninja Foodi will pause cooking when you open the baskets, so take advantage of this feature to give your food a quick toss or turn.

5. Not Adjusting for Wet Batters: Air fryers work best with dry coatings or breaded items. Wet batters can drip through the crisper plate, causing a mess and uneven cooking. If you're craving something like tempura, consider using a dry breadcrumb coating instead of a wet batter. Alternatively, freeze battered items for a short time before air frying to help them hold their shape.

6. Ignoring the Clean-Up: Regular cleaning is crucial to keeping your air fryer in top condition. After each use, make sure to clean the baskets and crisper plates to remove any food residue or grease. Allowing buildup to accumulate can affect the performance of your air fryer and potentially lead to unwanted flavors in your food. A clean air fryer is not only more efficient but also ensures that every meal you cook is as delicious as the last.

Adjusting Recipes for High Altitude or Different Climates

Cooking at high altitudes or in different climates can present unique challenges, but with a few adjustments, your Ninja Foodi 2-Basket Air Fryer can still deliver outstanding results. Here are some tips for adapting your recipes based on your environment:

1. High Altitude Cooking: At higher altitudes, the air pressure is lower, which affects the cooking process. Water boils at a lower temperature, and foods can take longer to cook. To compensate, you may need to increase the cooking time or temperature slightly. Start by adding an extra 2-5 minutes of cooking time and check for doneness. If needed, increase the temperature by 10-15°F (5-8°C) to achieve the desired results.

2. Dry Climates: In arid environments, foods can dry out more quickly during cooking. To prevent this, consider reducing the cooking time or using a lower temperature. You can also add a small amount of moisture to the food, such as a light brush of oil or a spritz of water, to help retain juiciness.

3. Humid Climates: High humidity can make it difficult to achieve that perfect crisp in your air-fried foods. In this case, it's important to use a slightly higher temperature to help evaporate the moisture on the surface of the food. Additionally, you may want to reduce the amount of oil used, as humidity can cause oil to cling to the food, leading to a greasy texture.

4. Seasonal Variations: Keep in mind that seasonal changes in temperature and humidity can also impact cooking times. During colder months, your kitchen might be cooler, which can affect the preheating time and overall cooking time. Similarly, in warmer months, foods may cook faster than expected. Always monitor your food closely and be prepared to make small adjustments to time and temperature as needed.

Dealing with Uneven Cooking: Solutions and Tips

Uneven cooking is a common concern, especially when you're just getting started with your Ninja Foodi 2-Basket Air Fryer. If you notice that some parts of your food are cooking faster than others, here are some solutions to help you achieve consistent results:

1. Ensure Proper Air Circulation: The key to even cooking in an air fryer is proper air circulation. If your food is too crowded or piled on top of each other, the hot air won't be able to reach every surface. Always arrange your food in a single layer and avoid stacking items unless the recipe specifically calls for it. If you're cooking a large quantity, it's better to cook in batches.

2. Use the Right Basket: The Ninja Foodi comes with crisper plates that allow hot air to circulate beneath the food as well as around it. Make sure you're using these plates correctly, as placing food directly in the baskets without the plates can block airflow and result in uneven cooking.

3. Rotate the Baskets: If you're cooking different foods in each basket, you may notice that one basket cooks faster than the other due to the differences in food type or quantity. To counteract this, try rotating the baskets halfway through the cooking time. This simple step can help ensure that both baskets cook evenly.

4. Adjust the Temperature: If one side of your food is browning too quickly while the other remains undercooked, you may need to lower the temperature slightly and extend the cooking time. This allows the food to cook through without burning the exterior. Remember that every food and recipe is different, so it might take a few tries to find the perfect temperature and time for your specific dish.

5. Preheat the Air Fryer: Preheating the Ninja Foodi ensures that the baskets are evenly heated before you start cooking. This can help reduce the chances of uneven cooking, especially for foods that require a crispy exterior. If you're cooking items that benefit from a sear or initial blast of heat, preheating is particularly important.

Cleaning and Maintaining Your Air Fryer: Prolonging Its Life

Proper cleaning and maintenance are essential for keeping your Ninja Foodi 2-Basket Air Fryer in optimal condition. Regular upkeep not only extends the life of your appliance but also ensures that every meal you cook is safe and delicious. Here's how to keep your air fryer clean and well-maintained:

1. Clean After Every Use: It's important to clean the baskets, crisper plates, and any removable parts after each use. This prevents food residue and grease from building up, which can affect the performance of the air fryer and lead to unwanted flavors in your food. Use warm, soapy water and a non-abrasive sponge or cloth to clean these parts. Make sure they're completely dry before reassembling the air fryer.

2. Wipe Down the Exterior: Don't forget to clean the exterior of the air fryer as well. Use a damp cloth to wipe down the outside, including the control panel. Avoid using harsh chemicals or abrasive materials, as these can damage the finish.

3. Check for Grease Buildup: Over time, grease can accumulate in the heating element or the vent areas. Periodically check these areas and clean them as needed to prevent smoke and ensure efficient cooking. A soft brush or cloth can be used to gently clean around the heating element.

4. Use Parchment Paper or Liners: To reduce mess and make cleanup easier, consider using perforated parchment paper or air fryer liners in the baskets. These liners allow air to circulate while preventing food from sticking to the crisper plates. Just be sure to use liners that are specifically designed for air fryers and that fit your baskets properly.

5. Deep Clean Occasionally: In addition to your regular cleaning routine, it's a good idea to give your air fryer a deeper clean every few weeks. This involves cleaning the interior of the unit, including the heating element, with a damp cloth or sponge. You can also soak the baskets and crisper plates in warm, soapy water for a more thorough clean.

6. Avoid Using Metal Utensils: To protect the non-stick coating on your air fryer baskets and crisper plates, avoid using metal utensils or abrasive sponges. Instead, opt for silicone, wooden, or plastic utensils that won't scratch the surface.

7. Store Properly: When not in use, store your Ninja Foodi in a clean, dry place. If you're not using it frequently, consider covering it with a cloth or dust cover to keep it free from dust and debris.

By following these cleaning and maintenance tips, you'll keep your Ninja Foodi 2-Basket Air Fryer in top condition, ensuring that it continues to deliver delicious, evenly cooked meals for years to come.

Frequently Asked Questions from Ninja Foodi Users

As you start using your Ninja Foodi 2-Basket Air Fryer, you might encounter a few questions or need clarification on certain aspects of the appliance. Here are some of the most common questions from users, along with helpful answers to guide you:

1. Can I use aluminum foil or parchment paper in my Ninja Foodi?

Yes, you can use aluminum foil or parchment paper in your Ninja Foodi 2-Basket Air Fryer. However, it's important to ensure that the foil or paper is securely placed in the basket and doesn't block the air vents. This allows for proper air circulation and prevents the foil or paper from being blown around by the hot air. Perforated parchment paper specifically designed for air fryers is a great option as it allows for even airflow while minimizing mess.

2. Why is my food not as crispy as I expected?

If your food isn't as crispy as you'd like, there could be a few reasons for this. First, make sure you're not overcrowding the baskets, as this can prevent the hot air from circulating properly. Additionally, check that you're using the correct temperature and time settings for the food you're cooking. If you're cooking frozen foods, consider adding a minute or two to the cooking time. Finally, a light mist of oil can help achieve a crispier texture, especially for breaded or coated items.

3. How do I prevent my air fryer from smoking?

Smoking can occur if there's excess grease or oil in the baskets or if food particles come into contact with the heating element. To prevent this, clean the baskets and crisper plates thoroughly after each use. If you're cooking fatty foods, like bacon or sausage, consider placing a small amount of water in the bottom of the basket to catch the grease. Additionally, avoid using too much oil, as this can cause smoking during cooking.

4. Can I cook frozen foods in the Ninja Foodi 2-Basket Air Fryer?

Absolutely! The Ninja Foodi is excellent for cooking frozen foods. You may need to adjust the cooking time slightly, adding a few extra minutes to ensure the food is heated through and reaches the desired crispiness. There's no need to thaw frozen foods before air frying, which makes this appliance perfect for quick and convenient meals.

5. How do I know when my food is done?

The best way to determine if your food is done is by checking it visually and using a food thermometer for meats. The Ninja Foodi's baskets can be opened during cooking without affecting the process, so feel free to check on your food as it cooks. For meats, ensure that they reach the recommended internal temperature: 165°F (74°C) for poultry, 145°F (63°C) for pork and fish, and 160°F (71°C) for ground meats.

6. Can I bake in my Ninja Foodi 2-Basket Air Fryer?

Yes, you can bake in your Ninja Foodi! The air fryer's baking function is perfect for making small batches of baked goods like muffins, cakes, or cookies. Just be sure to use oven-safe dishes or silicone molds that fit in the baskets. The baking function is also great for making desserts like brownies or cobblers, offering a quick and easy alternative to using your traditional oven.

By addressing these common questions and concerns, you'll feel more confident using your Ninja Foodi 2-Basket Air Fryer and be able to troubleshoot any issues that arise. This appliance is designed to make your cooking experience easier and more enjoyable, and with the right knowledge, you can maximize its potential in your kitchen.

Section 2: Mouth-Watering Recipes

Chapter 6: Breakfasts Made Easy

Making breakfast has never been easier or more enjoyable than with the Ninja Foodi 2-Basket Air Fryer. Whether you're craving something savory, sweet, or a combination of both, these recipes are designed to help you whip up delicious and nutritious meals quickly. The DualZone technology allows you to prepare multiple components at once, streamlining your morning routine. Let's dive into ten delightful breakfast recipes that are sure to become your morning staples.

1. Crispy Bacon and Fluffy Scrambled Eggs

A classic breakfast duo made effortlessly with the Ninja Foodi, offering perfectly crispy bacon and light, fluffy scrambled eggs.

Servings: 2
Preparation Time: 5 minutes
Cooking Time: 12 minutes
Ingredients:
- 4 strips of bacon
- 4 large eggs
- 2 tablespoons milk (30 ml)
- Salt and pepper to taste
- 1 tablespoon butter (optional)

Directions:
1. Preheat the Ninja Foodi to 400°F (200°C).
2. Place the bacon strips in one basket, making sure they are laid flat. Air fry for 10-12 minutes, depending on desired crispiness.
3. In a bowl, whisk together eggs, milk, salt, and pepper.
4. In the second basket, place a silicone baking dish or parchment paper, and pour in the egg mixture. Add butter if desired for creamier eggs. Air fry at 300°F (150°C) for 8-10 minutes, stirring halfway through.
5. Serve the crispy bacon alongside the scrambled eggs for a hearty breakfast.

2. Sweet Potato Breakfast Hash

A nutritious and filling hash with sweet potatoes, bell peppers, and onions, topped with a perfectly cooked egg.

Servings: 4
Preparation Time: 10 minutes
Cooking Time: 20 minutes
Ingredients:
- 2 medium sweet potatoes, peeled and diced
- 1 red bell pepper, diced
- 1 green bell pepper, diced
- 1 small onion, diced
- 2 tablespoons olive oil (30 ml)
- 1/2 teaspoon smoked paprika (2.5 g)
- Salt and pepper to taste
- 4 large eggs

Directions:
1. Preheat the Ninja Foodi to 390°F (200°C).
2. Toss the sweet potatoes, bell peppers, and onion with olive oil, smoked paprika, salt, and pepper in one basket. Air fry for 15-20 minutes, shaking halfway through.

3. In the second basket, crack each egg into a silicone mold. Air fry at 320°F (160°C) for 6-8 minutes until the whites are set.
4. Serve the hash with an egg on top for a balanced breakfast.

3. Blueberry Pancakes

Fluffy pancakes filled with juicy blueberries, cooked to perfection and ideal for a sweet morning treat.

Servings: 4
Preparation Time: 10 minutes
Cooking Time: 8 minutes
Ingredients:
- 1 cup all-purpose flour (120 g)
- 1 tablespoon sugar (15 g)
- 1 teaspoon baking powder (5 g)
- 1/2 teaspoon baking soda (2.5 g)
- 1/4 teaspoon salt (1.5 g)
- 1 large egg
- 3/4 cup milk (180 ml)
- 2 tablespoons melted butter (30 ml)
- 1/2 cup fresh or frozen blueberries (75 g)

Directions:
1. Preheat the Ninja Foodi to 350°F (175°C).
2. Whisk flour, sugar, baking powder, baking soda, and salt in a bowl. In another bowl, whisk together egg, milk, and melted butter. Combine the wet and dry ingredients, then fold in blueberries.
3. Pour batter into a silicone mold or parchment paper in one basket. Air fry for 6-8 minutes until golden brown.
4. Serve hot, topped with maple syrup and extra blueberries if desired.

4. Avocado Toast with Poached Eggs

A healthy and satisfying breakfast featuring creamy avocado and perfectly poached eggs atop crunchy toast.

Servings: 2
Preparation Time: 5 minutes
Cooking Time: 10 minutes
Ingredients:
- 2 slices of whole-grain bread
- 1 ripe avocado, mashed
- 2 large eggs
- 1 tablespoon white vinegar (15 ml)
- Salt, pepper, and red pepper flakes to taste

Directions:
1. Preheat the Ninja Foodi to 350°F (175°C).
2. In one basket, add water and vinegar to a silicone mold, crack an egg into each mold, and air fry at 320°F (160°C) for 8-10 minutes.
3. In the second basket, air fry the bread slices at 350°F (175°C) for 3-4 minutes until toasted.
4. Spread mashed avocado on the toast, top with poached eggs, and season with salt, pepper, and red pepper flakes.

5. Breakfast Sausage Patties

Homemade sausage patties seasoned to perfection and cooked crisp on the outside, juicy on the inside.

Servings: 4
Preparation Time: 10 minutes
Cooking Time: 8 minutes
Ingredients:
- 1 lb ground pork (450 g)
- 1 teaspoon dried sage (5 g)
- 1 teaspoon dried thyme (5 g)
- 1/2 teaspoon garlic powder (2.5 g)
- 1/2 teaspoon onion powder (2.5 g)
- 1/2 teaspoon salt (2.5 g)
- 1/4 teaspoon black pepper (1.5 g)
- 1/4 teaspoon red pepper flakes (optional)

Directions:
1. Preheat the Ninja Foodi to 375°F (190°C).
2. Mix ground pork with sage, thyme, garlic powder, onion powder, salt, pepper, and red pepper flakes. Form into 8 small patties.
3. Place patties in one basket, ensuring they don't overlap. Air fry for 6-8 minutes, flipping halfway through.
4. Serve with eggs, toast, or as part of a breakfast sandwich.

6. Veggie Omelet

A fluffy omelet packed with your favorite veggies, cooked evenly and quickly in the Ninja Foodi.
Servings: 2
Preparation Time: 5 minutes
Cooking Time: 10 minutes
Ingredients:
- 4 large eggs
- 1/4 cup milk (60 ml)
- 1/2 cup diced bell peppers (75 g)
- 1/4 cup diced onion (35 g)
- 1/4 cup sliced mushrooms (35 g)
- 1/4 cup shredded cheese (30 g)
- Salt and pepper to taste

Directions:
1. Preheat the Ninja Foodi to 320°F (160°C).
2. In one basket, air fry bell peppers, onion, and mushrooms for 5-7 minutes until softened.
3. Whisk eggs, milk, salt, and pepper in a bowl. Pour egg mixture into a silicone mold or parchment paper in the second basket.
4. Add cooked vegetables to the eggs and air fry for another 8-10 minutes. Sprinkle cheese on top during the last 2 minutes of cooking.
5. Serve hot, folded in half.

7. Cinnamon Sugar French Toast Sticks

Crispy on the outside, soft on the inside, these cinnamon sugar-coated French toast sticks are a fun and tasty breakfast treat.
Servings: 4
Preparation Time: 10 minutes
Cooking Time: 8 minutes
Ingredients:
- 4 slices of thick-cut bread
- 2 large eggs
- 1/2 cup milk (120 ml)
- 1 teaspoon vanilla extract (5 ml)
- 1/4 cup sugar (50 g)
- 1 teaspoon ground cinnamon (5 g)
- Butter or cooking spray for greasing

Directions:
1. Preheat the Ninja Foodi to 350°F (175°C).
2. Cut each slice of bread into 3-4 sticks.
3. Whisk eggs, milk, and vanilla extract. In a separate bowl, mix sugar and cinnamon.
4. Dip bread sticks into egg mixture, allowing excess to drip off. Grease one basket with butter or cooking spray, place sticks in the basket, and air fry for 6-8 minutes, flipping halfway through.
5. Immediately toss hot French toast sticks in the cinnamon sugar mixture. Serve with syrup for dipping.

8. Mini Quiche Lorraine

Delightful mini quiches filled with bacon, cheese, and a rich egg custard, perfect for breakfast or brunch.
Servings: 4
Preparation Time: 10 minutes
Cooking Time: 12 minutes
Ingredients:
- 4 large eggs
- 1/2 cup heavy cream (120 ml)
- 4 slices bacon, cooked and crumbled
- 1/2 cup shredded Swiss cheese (60 g)
- Salt and pepper to taste
- 1 pre-made pie crust (optional, for added texture)

Directions:
1. Preheat the Ninja Foodi to 350°F (175°C).
2. Whisk eggs, heavy cream, salt, and pepper in a bowl. Stir in crumbled bacon and cheese.
3. If using a pie crust, cut it to fit silicone muffin molds. Press crust into molds, then pour egg mixture on top.
4. Place molds in one basket and air fry for 10-12 minutes until quiches are set and golden.
5. Cool slightly before removing from molds and serve warm.

9. Banana Nut Muffins

Moist and flavorful banana nut muffins, perfect for a quick breakfast or snack on the go.
Servings: 6
Preparation Time: 10 minutes
Cooking Time: 15 minutes
Ingredients:
- 2 ripe bananas, mashed

- 1/4 cup melted butter (60 ml)
- 1/4 cup sugar (50 g)
- 1 large egg
- 1 teaspoon vanilla extract (5 ml)
- 1 cup all-purpose flour (120 g)
- 1/2 teaspoon baking soda (2.5 g)
- 1/4 teaspoon salt (1.5 g)
- 1/4 cup chopped walnuts (30 g)

Directions:

1. Preheat the Ninja Foodi to 350°F (175°C).
2. Combine mashed bananas, melted butter, sugar, egg, and vanilla extract in a bowl. Stir in flour, baking soda, and salt until just combined. Fold in walnuts.
3. Spoon batter into silicone muffin molds. Place molds in one basket and air fry for 12-15 minutes, or until a toothpick inserted comes out clean.
4. Cool slightly before removing from molds. Serve warm or at room temperature.

10. Breakfast Burritos

A hearty breakfast burrito stuffed with scrambled eggs, cheese, sausage, and veggies, perfect for a filling start to your day.

Servings: 4
Preparation Time: 10 minutes
Cooking Time: 12 minutes
Ingredients:

- 4 large flour tortillas
- 6 large eggs
- 1/4 cup milk (60 ml)
- 1/2 cup cooked sausage crumbles (75 g)
- 1/2 cup shredded cheddar cheese (60 g)
- 1/4 cup diced bell peppers (35 g)
- 1/4 cup diced onions (35 g)
- Salt and pepper to taste

Directions:

1. Preheat the Ninja Foodi to 350°F (175°C).
2. In one basket, air fry bell peppers and onions for 5-7 minutes until softened.
3. Whisk eggs, milk, salt, and pepper in a bowl. Pour egg mixture into a silicone mold in the second basket and air fry at 300°F (150°C) for 8-10 minutes, stirring halfway through.
4. Layer scrambled eggs, sausage, vegetables, and cheese on each tortilla. Roll up tightly.
5. Place burritos in one basket and air fry at 350°F (175°C) for 3-4 minutes until heated through.
6. Serve immediately or wrap in foil for a grab-and-go breakfast.

11. Apple Cinnamon Oatmeal

Warm, comforting oatmeal infused with apples and cinnamon, perfect for a cozy start to your day.

Servings: 2
Preparation Time: 5 minutes
Cooking Time: 15 minutes
Ingredients:

- 1 cup rolled oats (90 g)
- 2 cups water or milk (480 ml)
- 1 apple, peeled and diced
- 1 teaspoon ground cinnamon (5 g)
- 1 tablespoon honey or maple syrup (15 ml)
- 1/4 cup chopped walnuts (30 g) (optional)

Directions:

1. Preheat the Ninja Foodi to 350°F (175°C).
2. In one basket, mix oats, water or milk, diced apple, and cinnamon. Air fry for 12-15 minutes, stirring halfway through, until oats are tender.
3. Stir in honey or maple syrup and top with walnuts if desired. Serve warm.

12. Spinach and Feta Breakfast Wraps

A delicious and healthy breakfast wrap filled with spinach, feta, and scrambled eggs, perfect for a quick and satisfying meal.

Servings: 4
Preparation Time: 10 minutes
Cooking Time: 12 minutes
Ingredients:

- 4 large flour tortillas
- 4 large eggs
- 1/4 cup milk (60 ml)
- 1 cup fresh spinach (30 g)
- 1/4 cup crumbled feta cheese (60 g)
- Salt and pepper to taste

Directions:

1. Preheat the Ninja Foodi to 320°F (160°C).

2. In one basket, air fry spinach for 3-4 minutes until wilted.
3. Whisk eggs, milk, salt, and pepper in a bowl. Pour egg mixture into a silicone mold in the second basket and air fry at 300°F (150°C) for 8-10 minutes, stirring halfway through.
4. Divide the scrambled eggs, wilted spinach, and feta among the tortillas. Roll up tightly.
5. Serve the wraps immediately or wrap in foil for a grab-and-go option.

13. Chocolate Chip Banana Bread

A moist and flavorful banana bread studded with chocolate chips, perfect for breakfast or a snack.
Servings: 6
Preparation Time: 10 minutes
Cooking Time: 20 minutes
Ingredients:
- 2 ripe bananas, mashed
- 1/4 cup melted butter (60 ml)
- 1/4 cup sugar (50 g)
- 1 large egg
- 1 teaspoon vanilla extract (5 ml)
- 1 cup all-purpose flour (120 g)
- 1/2 teaspoon baking soda (2.5 g)
- 1/4 teaspoon salt (1.5 g)
- 1/2 cup chocolate chips (85 g)

Directions:
1. Preheat the Ninja Foodi to 350°F (175°C).
2. In a bowl, combine mashed bananas, melted butter, sugar, egg, and vanilla extract. Stir in flour, baking soda, and salt until just combined. Fold in chocolate chips.
3. Pour the batter into a silicone loaf pan or parchment paper in one basket. Air fry for 18-20 minutes, or until a toothpick inserted comes out clean.
4. Allow the banana bread to cool slightly before slicing and serving.

14. Ham and Cheese Breakfast Croissants

Flaky croissants filled with ham and cheese, perfect for a quick and indulgent breakfast.
Servings: 4
Preparation Time: 5 minutes
Cooking Time: 10 minutes
Ingredients:
- 4 pre-made croissant dough pieces
- 4 slices of ham
- 4 slices of Swiss or cheddar cheese

Directions:
1. Preheat the Ninja Foodi to 350°F (175°C).
2. Roll out each croissant dough piece and place a slice of ham and cheese in the center. Roll up the dough, sealing the edges.
3. Place the croissants in one basket, seam side down, and air fry for 8-10 minutes until golden brown and flaky.
4. Serve warm, straight from the air fryer.

15. Sweet Potato and Black Bean Breakfast Tacos

These tacos are a flavorful and filling way to start your day, featuring roasted sweet potatoes, black beans, and a fried egg.
Servings: 4
Preparation Time: 10 minutes
Cooking Time: 20 minutes
Ingredients:
- 2 medium sweet potatoes, peeled and diced
- 1 tablespoon olive oil (15 ml)
- 1/2 teaspoon cumin (2.5 g)
- 1/2 teaspoon smoked paprika (2.5 g)
- Salt and pepper to taste
- 1 cup canned black beans, drained and rinsed (170 g)
- 4 large eggs
- 4 small corn or flour tortillas

Directions:
1. Preheat the Ninja Foodi to 390°F (200°C).
2. Toss diced sweet potatoes with olive oil, cumin, smoked paprika, salt, and pepper in one basket. Air fry for 15-20 minutes until tender and lightly browned.

3. In the second basket, crack the eggs and air fry at 320°F (160°C) for 6-8 minutes, until whites are set but yolks remain runny.
4. Warm the tortillas and assemble the tacos with sweet potatoes, black beans, and a fried egg on top.
5. Serve immediately with your favorite salsa or hot sauce.

16. Mushroom and Swiss Cheese Frittata

A light and fluffy frittata packed with savory mushrooms and creamy Swiss cheese.
Servings: 4
Preparation Time: 10 minutes
Cooking Time: 15 minutes
Ingredients:
- 6 large eggs
- 1/4 cup milk (60 ml)
- 1 cup sliced mushrooms (70 g)
- 1/2 cup shredded Swiss cheese (60 g)
- 1/4 teaspoon salt (1.5 g)
- 1/4 teaspoon black pepper (1.5 g)
- 1 tablespoon olive oil (15 ml)

Directions:
1. Preheat the Ninja Foodi to 350°F (175°C).
2. In one basket, toss mushrooms with olive oil and air fry for 5-7 minutes until tender.
3. Whisk together eggs, milk, salt, and pepper in a bowl. Pour egg mixture into a silicone mold or parchment paper in the second basket.
4. Add cooked mushrooms and sprinkle with Swiss cheese. Air fry for 12-15 minutes until the frittata is fully set and lightly golden.
5. Slice and serve warm.

17. Greek Yogurt Parfait

A refreshing and healthy breakfast parfait layered with Greek yogurt, fresh berries, and granola.
Servings: 2
Preparation Time: 5 minutes
Cooking Time: 0 minutes
Ingredients:
- 2 cups Greek yogurt (450 g)
- 1 cup mixed berries (150 g)
- 1/2 cup granola (60 g)
- 1 tablespoon honey (15 ml)

Directions:
1. In a glass or bowl, layer 1/2 cup of Greek yogurt, followed by a handful of mixed berries and a sprinkle of granola.
2. Repeat the layers, finishing with a drizzle of honey on top.
3. Serve immediately for a fresh and nutritious breakfast.

18. Lemon Poppy Seed Muffins

Light and tangy muffins with a delightful crunch from poppy seeds, perfect for breakfast or a snack.
Servings: 6
Preparation Time: 10 minutes
Cooking Time: 15 minutes
Ingredients:
- 1 cup all-purpose flour (120 g)
- 1/2 cup sugar (100 g)
- 1/2 teaspoon baking powder (2.5 g)
- 1/4 teaspoon baking soda (1.5 g)
- 1/4 teaspoon salt (1.5 g)
- 1 tablespoon poppy seeds (15 g)
- 1/2 cup Greek yogurt (120 g)
- 1/4 cup melted butter (60 ml)
- 1 large egg
- 1 teaspoon lemon zest (5 g)
- 1 tablespoon lemon juice (15 ml)

Directions:
1. Preheat the Ninja Foodi to 350°F (175°C).
2. In a bowl, whisk together flour, sugar, baking powder, baking soda, salt, and poppy seeds.
3. In another bowl, combine Greek yogurt, melted butter, egg, lemon zest, and lemon juice. Add the wet ingredients to the dry ingredients and mix until just combined.
4. Spoon the batter into silicone muffin molds and place in one basket. Air fry for 12-15 minutes, or until a toothpick inserted comes out clean.
5. Let cool slightly before serving.

19. Savory Breakfast Quesadillas

Cheesy quesadillas filled with scrambled eggs, sausage, and veggies, perfect for a hearty breakfast.

Servings: 4
Preparation Time: 10 minutes
Cooking Time: 12 minutes
Ingredients:

- 4 large flour tortillas
- 6 large eggs
- 1/4 cup milk (60 ml)
- 1/2 cup cooked sausage crumbles (75 g)
- 1/2 cup shredded cheddar cheese (60 g)
- 1/4 cup diced bell peppers (35 g)
- 1/4 cup diced onions (35 g)
- Salt and pepper to taste

Directions:

1. Preheat the Ninja Foodi to 350°F (175°C).
2. In one basket, air fry bell peppers and onions for 5-7 minutes until softened.
3. Whisk eggs, milk, salt, and pepper in a bowl. Pour egg mixture into a silicone mold in the second basket and air fry at 300°F (150°C) for 8-10 minutes, stirring halfway through.
4. On each tortilla, layer scrambled eggs, sausage, vegetables, and cheese. Fold in half and place in the air fryer basket.
5. Air fry the quesadillas at 350°F (175°C) for 3-4 minutes, or until the cheese is melted and the tortillas are crispy.
6. Serve immediately with salsa or sour cream.

20. Zucchini Bread

A moist and flavorful bread made with fresh zucchini, perfect for breakfast or a snack.

Servings: 6
Preparation Time: 10 minutes
Cooking Time: 20 minutes
Ingredients:

- 1 cup grated zucchini (130 g)
- 1/2 cup melted butter (120 ml)
- 1/2 cup sugar (100 g)
- 1 large egg
- 1 teaspoon vanilla extract (5 ml)
- 1 1/2 cups all-purpose flour (180 g)
- 1/2 teaspoon baking soda (2.5 g)
- 1/2 teaspoon baking powder (2.5 g)
- 1/4 teaspoon salt (1.5 g)
- 1 teaspoon ground cinnamon (5 g)

Directions:

1. Preheat the Ninja Foodi to 350°F (175°C).
2. In a large bowl, whisk together melted butter, sugar, egg, and vanilla extract. Stir in grated zucchini.
3. In another bowl, mix flour, baking soda, baking powder, salt, and cinnamon. Gradually add the dry ingredients to the wet mixture, stirring until just combined.
4. Pour the batter into a silicone loaf pan or parchment paper in one basket. Air fry for 18-20 minutes, or until a toothpick inserted comes out clean.
5. Allow the zucchini bread to cool slightly before slicing and serving.

Chapter 7: Quick and Tasty Lunches

Lunchtime should be simple, flavorful, and nutritious. With the Ninja Foodi 2-Basket Air Fryer, you can prepare quick and delicious meals that don't compromise on taste or health. Whether you're in the mood for something light and fresh or hearty and satisfying, these ten recipes will inspire you to make the most of your lunch break. Each recipe is designed to be easy to follow, allowing you to create mouthwatering dishes with minimal effort.

1. Mediterranean Chicken Pita Pockets

Juicy, marinated chicken served in warm pita pockets with fresh veggies and tangy tzatziki sauce—a quick and healthy Mediterranean-inspired lunch.

Servings: 4

Preparation Time: 15 minutes (plus 30 minutes marinating)

Cooking Time: 12 minutes

Ingredients:

- 1 lb boneless, skinless chicken breasts, cut into strips (450 g)
- 2 tablespoons olive oil (30 ml)
- 2 tablespoons lemon juice (30 ml)
- 2 cloves garlic, minced
- 1 teaspoon dried oregano (5 g)
- 1/2 teaspoon salt (2.5 g)
- 1/2 teaspoon black pepper (2.5 g)
- 4 whole wheat pita pockets
- 1 cup chopped cucumber (150 g)
- 1 cup chopped tomatoes (150 g)
- 1/2 cup tzatziki sauce (120 ml)

Directions:

1. In a bowl, combine olive oil, lemon juice, garlic, oregano, salt, and pepper. Add the chicken strips and marinate for at least 30 minutes.
2. Preheat the Ninja Foodi to 375°F (190°C).
3. Place the marinated chicken in one basket and air fry for 10-12 minutes, turning halfway through until fully cooked.
4. Warm the pita pockets in the second basket at 350°F (175°C) for 2-3 minutes.
5. Fill each pita with chicken, cucumber, tomatoes, and a drizzle of tzatziki sauce. Serve immediately.

2. Caprese Stuffed Portobello Mushrooms

These hearty portobello mushrooms are stuffed with fresh mozzarella, tomatoes, and basil, making a satisfying and flavorful vegetarian lunch.

Servings: 4

Preparation Time: 10 minutes

Cooking Time: 15 minutes

Ingredients:

- 4 large portobello mushrooms, stems removed
- 8 oz fresh mozzarella, sliced (225 g)
- 2 medium tomatoes, sliced
- 1/4 cup fresh basil leaves (15 g)
- 2 tablespoons balsamic glaze (30 ml)
- Salt and pepper to taste

Directions:

1. Preheat the Ninja Foodi to 375°F (190°C).
2. Place the portobello mushrooms in one basket, cap side down. Air fry for 8 minutes until slightly softened.

3. Remove the mushrooms and layer each with mozzarella, tomato slices, and basil leaves.
4. Return the stuffed mushrooms to the basket and air fry for an additional 5-7 minutes until the cheese is melted.
5. Drizzle with balsamic glaze, season with salt and pepper, and serve warm.

3. Teriyaki Tofu Stir-Fry

Crispy tofu and tender vegetables coated in a flavorful teriyaki sauce make this a quick and healthy plant-based lunch option.
Servings: 4
Preparation Time: 10 minutes
Cooking Time: 15 minutes
Ingredients:
- 1 block firm tofu, pressed and cubed (14 oz, 400 g)
- 1 tablespoon cornstarch (15 g)
- 2 tablespoons soy sauce (30 ml)
- 1 tablespoon sesame oil (15 ml)
- 1 red bell pepper, sliced
- 1 zucchini, sliced
- 1 cup broccoli florets (150 g)
- 1/4 cup teriyaki sauce (60 ml)
- Cooked rice for serving

Directions:
1. Preheat the Ninja Foodi to 390°F (200°C).
2. Toss the tofu cubes in cornstarch and soy sauce. Place in one basket and air fry for 12-15 minutes, shaking halfway through until crispy.
3. In the second basket, air fry the bell pepper, zucchini, and broccoli at 375°F (190°C) for 8-10 minutes until tender.
4. Combine the crispy tofu and cooked vegetables in a bowl, toss with teriyaki sauce, and serve over rice.

4. BBQ Pulled Pork Sandwiches

Tender pulled pork smothered in BBQ sauce and served on a soft bun, perfect for a quick and comforting lunch.
Servings: 4
Preparation Time: 10 minutes
Cooking Time: 20 minutes

Ingredients:
- 1 lb pork tenderloin, cut into chunks (450 g)
- 1/2 cup BBQ sauce (120 ml)
- 4 sandwich buns
- 1/2 cup coleslaw (optional, 60 g)

Directions:
1. Preheat the Ninja Foodi to 375°F (190°C).
2. Place the pork chunks in one basket and air fry for 18-20 minutes until fully cooked and tender.
3. Shred the cooked pork with two forks and mix with BBQ sauce.
4. Toast the buns in the second basket at 350°F (175°C) for 2-3 minutes.
5. Assemble the sandwiches with pulled pork and coleslaw, if desired. Serve immediately.

5. Southwest Chicken Salad

A fresh and zesty salad featuring grilled chicken, black beans, corn, and avocado, all tossed in a lime-cilantro dressing.
Servings: 4
Preparation Time: 10 minutes
Cooking Time: 15 minutes
Ingredients:
- 1 lb boneless, skinless chicken breasts (450 g)
- 1 tablespoon olive oil (15 ml)
- 1 teaspoon chili powder (5 g)
- 1/2 teaspoon cumin (2.5 g)
- 1/2 teaspoon garlic powder (2.5 g)
- Salt and pepper to taste
- 4 cups mixed greens (120 g)
- 1 can black beans, drained and rinsed (15 oz, 425 g)
- 1 cup corn kernels (150 g)
- 1 avocado, sliced
- 1/4 cup chopped cilantro (15 g)
- Juice of 1 lime

Directions:
1. Preheat the Ninja Foodi to 375°F (190°C).
2. Rub the chicken breasts with olive oil, chili powder, cumin, garlic powder, salt, and pepper. Place in one basket and air fry for 12-15 minutes, flipping halfway through until fully cooked.

3. Let the chicken rest for a few minutes before slicing.
4. In a large bowl, toss the mixed greens with black beans, corn, avocado, cilantro, and lime juice.
5. Top the salad with sliced chicken and serve immediately.

6. Greek-Style Veggie Burgers

Delicious veggie burgers made with chickpeas, feta, and spinach, served in a pita with a side of tzatziki sauce.
Servings: 4
Preparation Time: 15 minutes
Cooking Time: 12 minutes
Ingredients:
- 1 can chickpeas, drained and rinsed (15 oz, 425 g)
- 1/4 cup breadcrumbs (30 g)
- 1/4 cup crumbled feta cheese (30 g)
- 1/2 cup chopped spinach (30 g)
- 1 small onion, finely chopped
- 1 teaspoon dried oregano (5 g)
- 1/2 teaspoon garlic powder (2.5 g)
- Salt and pepper to taste
- 4 whole wheat pitas
- 1/2 cup tzatziki sauce (120 ml)

Directions:
1. In a food processor, blend chickpeas, breadcrumbs, feta, spinach, onion, oregano, garlic powder, salt, and pepper until well combined but still slightly chunky.
2. Form the mixture into 4 patties.
3. Preheat the Ninja Foodi to 375°F (190°C).
4. Place the patties in one basket and air fry for 10-12 minutes until golden and firm, flipping halfway through.
5. Warm the pitas in the second basket at 350°F (175°C) for 1-2 minutes.
6. Serve the veggie burgers in pitas with a side of tzatziki sauce.

7. Shrimp Tacos with Mango Salsa

Fresh and flavorful shrimp tacos topped with a sweet and tangy mango salsa, perfect for a light and refreshing lunch.
Servings: 4
Preparation Time: 10 minutes
Cooking Time: 10 minutes
Ingredients:
- 1 lb large shrimp, peeled and deveined (450 g)
- 1 tablespoon olive oil (15 ml)
- 1 teaspoon chili powder (5 g)
- 1/2 teaspoon garlic powder (2.5 g)
- Salt and pepper to taste
- 8 small corn tortillas
- 1 ripe mango, diced
- 1/2 red onion, finely chopped
- 1/4 cup chopped cilantro (15 g)
- Juice of 1 lime

Directions:
1. Preheat the Ninja Foodi to 400°F (200°C).
2. Toss the shrimp with olive oil, chili powder, garlic powder, salt, and pepper. Place in one basket and air fry for 8-10 minutes until pink and cooked through.
3. In a bowl, combine mango, red onion, cilantro, and lime juice to make the salsa.
4. Warm the tortillas in the second basket at 350°F (175°C) for 1-2 minutes.
5. Serve the shrimp in tortillas topped with mango salsa. Enjoy immediately.

8. Turkey and Avocado Panini

A warm and satisfying panini filled with turkey, creamy avocado, and melted cheese, perfect for a quick lunch.
Servings: 4
Preparation Time: 5 minutes
Cooking Time: 10 minutes
Ingredients:
- 8 slices whole-grain bread
- 8 slices turkey breast (about 200 g)
- 1 avocado, sliced
- 4 slices provolone or Swiss cheese (about 100 g)
- 2 tablespoons Dijon mustard (30 ml)
- Olive oil for brushing

Directions:

1. Preheat the Ninja Foodi to 375°F (190°C).
2. Brush one side of each bread slice with olive oil. Spread Dijon mustard on the other side.
3. Layer turkey, avocado slices, and cheese on four slices of bread. Top with the remaining bread slices, olive oil side out.
4. Place the sandwiches in one basket and air fry for 8-10 minutes until the bread is golden and the cheese is melted, flipping halfway through.
5. Serve hot and enjoy.

9. Asian-Inspired Chicken Lettuce Wraps

Light and flavorful lettuce wraps filled with savory chicken, crunchy vegetables, and a tangy soy-ginger sauce.

Servings: 4
Preparation Time: 10 minutes
Cooking Time: 10 minutes
Ingredients:

- 1 lb ground chicken (450 g)
- 1 tablespoon sesame oil (15 ml)
- 2 cloves garlic, minced
- 1 tablespoon fresh ginger, grated (15 g)
- 2 tablespoons soy sauce (30 ml)
- 1 tablespoon hoisin sauce (15 ml)
- 1/4 cup chopped water chestnuts (35 g)
- 1/4 cup shredded carrots (35 g)
- 8 large lettuce leaves (such as butter or iceberg)

Directions:

1. Preheat the Ninja Foodi to 375°F (190°C).
2. In a skillet, heat sesame oil over medium heat. Add garlic and ginger, and cook until fragrant, about 1 minute.
3. Add ground chicken and cook until browned. Stir in soy sauce, hoisin sauce, water chestnuts, and carrots. Cook for another 2-3 minutes until heated through.
4. Spoon the chicken mixture into lettuce leaves and serve immediately.

10. Spicy Beef and Black Bean Burritos

A hearty and flavorful burrito filled with spiced beef, black beans, and melted cheese, wrapped in a warm tortilla.

Servings: 4
Preparation Time: 10 minutes
Cooking Time: 15 minutes
Ingredients:

- 1 lb ground beef (450 g)
- 1 tablespoon olive oil (15 ml)
- 1 teaspoon chili powder (5 g)
- 1/2 teaspoon cumin (2.5 g)
- 1/2 teaspoon garlic powder (2.5 g)
- Salt and pepper to taste
- 1 can black beans, drained and rinsed (15 oz, 425 g)
- 1 cup shredded cheddar cheese (120 g)
- 4 large flour tortillas
- 1/4 cup salsa (60 ml)
- 1/4 cup sour cream (60 ml) (optional)

Directions:

1. Preheat the Ninja Foodi to 375°F (190°C).
2. In a skillet, heat olive oil over medium heat. Add ground beef, chili powder, cumin, garlic powder, salt, and pepper. Cook until beef is browned.
3. Stir in black beans and cook for another 2-3 minutes until heated through.
4. Warm the tortillas in one basket at 350°F (175°C) for 2-3 minutes.
5. Fill each tortilla with the beef and bean mixture, top with cheddar cheese, and roll up into a burrito.
6. If desired, air fry the assembled burritos in the second basket at 350°F (175°C) for 3-4 minutes to melt the cheese and crisp the tortillas. Serve with salsa and sour cream.

11. Margherita Flatbread

A simple yet delicious flatbread topped with fresh tomatoes, mozzarella, and basil for a quick and satisfying lunch.

Servings: 4
Preparation Time: 10 minutes
Cooking Time: 10 minutes
Ingredients:

- 2 store-bought flatbreads
- 1/2 cup marinara sauce (120 ml)
- 8 oz fresh mozzarella, sliced (225 g)
- 2 medium tomatoes, sliced
- 1/4 cup fresh basil leaves (15 g)
- 1 tablespoon olive oil (15 ml)
- Salt and pepper to taste

Directions:

1. Preheat the Ninja Foodi to 375°F (190°C).
2. Spread marinara sauce evenly over the flatbreads. Top with mozzarella slices and tomato slices.
3. Place the flatbreads in one basket and air fry for 8-10 minutes until the cheese is melted and bubbly.
4. Remove from the air fryer, sprinkle with fresh basil leaves, drizzle with olive oil, and season with salt and pepper. Slice and serve warm.

12. Buffalo Cauliflower Bites

Crispy and spicy buffalo cauliflower bites served with a side of ranch dressing, perfect for a light and flavorful lunch.

Servings: 4
Preparation Time: 10 minutes
Cooking Time: 15 minutes
Ingredients:

- 1 medium head of cauliflower, cut into florets
- 1/2 cup all-purpose flour (60 g)
- 1/2 cup water (120 ml)
- 1/2 teaspoon garlic powder (2.5 g)
- 1/2 teaspoon paprika (2.5 g)
- Salt and pepper to taste
- 1/2 cup buffalo sauce (120 ml)
- 1/4 cup ranch dressing (60 ml) for serving

Directions:

1. Preheat the Ninja Foodi to 390°F (200°C).
2. In a bowl, whisk together flour, water, garlic powder, paprika, salt, and pepper to create a batter. Toss the cauliflower florets in the batter until evenly coated.
3. Place the coated cauliflower in one basket and air fry for 12-15 minutes until crispy, shaking the basket halfway through.
4. Toss the cooked cauliflower in buffalo sauce and serve immediately with ranch dressing on the side.

13. Chicken and Avocado Salad Wraps

A healthy and refreshing wrap filled with grilled chicken, creamy avocado, and fresh greens.

Servings: 4
Preparation Time: 10 minutes
Cooking Time: 15 minutes
Ingredients:

- 1 lb boneless, skinless chicken breasts (450 g)
- 1 tablespoon olive oil (15 ml)
- 1 teaspoon garlic powder (5 g)
- Salt and pepper to taste
- 4 large whole wheat tortillas
- 1 avocado, sliced
- 1 cup mixed greens (30 g)
- 1/4 cup ranch dressing (60 ml)

Directions:

1. Preheat the Ninja Foodi to 375°F (190°C).
2. Rub the chicken breasts with olive oil, garlic powder, salt, and pepper. Place in one basket and air fry for 12-15 minutes, flipping halfway through until fully cooked.
3. Let the chicken rest for a few minutes before slicing into thin strips.
4. Warm the tortillas in the second basket at 350°F (175°C) for 1-2 minutes.
5. Assemble the wraps by layering chicken, avocado, mixed greens, and ranch dressing on each tortilla. Roll up tightly and serve immediately.

14. Mediterranean Quinoa Salad

A light and refreshing quinoa salad with cucumbers, tomatoes, olives, and feta, perfect for a quick and healthy lunch.

Servings: 4
Preparation Time: 10 minutes
Cooking Time: 15 minutes
Ingredients:

- 1 cup quinoa (180 g)
- 2 cups water (480 ml)
- 1 cucumber, diced
- 1 cup cherry tomatoes, halved (150 g)
- 1/4 cup kalamata olives, sliced (30 g)
- 1/4 cup crumbled feta cheese (30 g)
- 2 tablespoons olive oil (30 ml)
- Juice of 1 lemon
- Salt and pepper to taste

Directions:

1. Rinse the quinoa under cold water. In a saucepan, bring quinoa and water to a boil. Reduce heat, cover, and simmer for 12-15 minutes until water is absorbed and quinoa is fluffy.
2. In a large bowl, combine cooked quinoa, cucumber, cherry tomatoes, olives, and feta cheese.
3. Drizzle with olive oil and lemon juice, then toss to combine. Season with salt and pepper to taste.
4. Serve chilled or at room temperature.

15. Italian Meatball Subs

Juicy meatballs smothered in marinara sauce and melted mozzarella, served in a toasted sub roll for a hearty and satisfying lunch.

Servings: 4
Preparation Time: 10 minutes
Cooking Time: 20 minutes
Ingredients:

- 1 lb ground beef (450 g)
- 1/4 cup breadcrumbs (30 g)
- 1/4 cup grated Parmesan cheese (30 g)
- 1 egg
- 1 teaspoon dried oregano (5 g)
- 1/2 teaspoon garlic powder (2.5 g)
- Salt and pepper to taste
- 1 cup marinara sauce (240 ml)
- 4 sub rolls
- 1 cup shredded mozzarella cheese (120 g)

Directions:

1. Preheat the Ninja Foodi to 375°F (190°C).
2. In a bowl, combine ground beef, breadcrumbs, Parmesan cheese, egg, oregano, garlic powder, salt, and pepper. Mix well and form into 12 meatballs.
3. Place the meatballs in one basket and air fry for 15 minutes until browned and cooked through.
4. Warm the marinara sauce in a saucepan over medium heat. Add the cooked meatballs to the sauce and simmer for a few minutes.
5. Toast the sub rolls in the second basket at 350°F (175°C) for 2-3 minutes.
6. Assemble the subs by placing meatballs in the rolls, spooning marinara sauce over the top, and sprinkling with mozzarella cheese. Serve hot.

16. Crispy Chickpea Tacos

Crunchy chickpeas spiced with cumin and chili powder, served in soft tortillas with fresh toppings.

Servings: 4
Preparation Time: 10 minutes
Cooking Time: 15 minutes
Ingredients:

- 1 can chickpeas, drained and rinsed (15 oz, 425 g)
- 1 tablespoon olive oil (15 ml)
- 1 teaspoon cumin (5 g)
- 1 teaspoon chili powder (5 g)
- Salt and pepper to taste
- 8 small corn tortillas
- 1/2 cup shredded lettuce (30 g)
- 1/2 cup diced tomatoes (75 g)
- 1/4 cup sour cream (60 ml)

Directions:

1. Preheat the Ninja Foodi to 390°F (200°C).
2. Toss the chickpeas with olive oil, cumin, chili powder, salt, and pepper. Place in one basket

and air fry for 12-15 minutes until crispy, shaking halfway through.

3. Warm the tortillas in the second basket at 350°F (175°C) for 1-2 minutes.

4. Fill each tortilla with crispy chickpeas, lettuce, tomatoes, and a dollop of sour cream. Serve immediately.

17. Grilled Halloumi and Veggie Skewers

Chewy halloumi cheese and a variety of vegetables grilled to perfection and served with a zesty lemon dressing.

Servings: 4
Preparation Time: 15 minutes
Cooking Time: 12 minutes
Ingredients:

- 8 oz halloumi cheese, cut into cubes (225 g)
- 1 red bell pepper, cut into chunks
- 1 zucchini, sliced
- 1 red onion, cut into wedges
- 2 tablespoons olive oil (30 ml)
- 1 tablespoon lemon juice (15 ml)
- 1 teaspoon dried oregano (5 g)
- Salt and pepper to taste
- Wooden or metal skewers

Directions:

1. Preheat the Ninja Foodi to 375°F (190°C).
2. In a bowl, toss the halloumi, bell pepper, zucchini, and onion with olive oil, lemon juice, oregano, salt, and pepper.
3. Thread the halloumi and vegetables onto skewers.
4. Place the skewers in one basket and air fry for 10-12 minutes, turning halfway through until the vegetables are tender and the cheese is golden.
5. Serve the skewers hot with additional lemon juice if desired.

18. Tuna Salad Stuffed Avocados

A creamy tuna salad served in avocado halves for a light and nutritious lunch.

Servings: 4
Preparation Time: 10 minutes
Cooking Time: 0 minutes
Ingredients:

- 2 cans tuna in water, drained (10 oz, 280 g total)
- 1/4 cup mayonnaise (60 ml)
- 1 tablespoon Dijon mustard (15 ml)
- 1/4 cup diced celery (30 g)
- 1/4 cup diced red onion (35 g)
- 2 avocados, halved and pitted
- Salt and pepper to taste
- 1 tablespoon chopped fresh parsley (optional, 5 g)

Directions:

1. In a bowl, combine tuna, mayonnaise, Dijon mustard, celery, red onion, salt, and pepper. Mix well.
2. Scoop the tuna salad into the avocado halves.
3. Garnish with chopped fresh parsley if desired. Serve immediately.

19. Garlic Parmesan Chicken Wings

Crispy chicken wings coated in a savory garlic Parmesan sauce, perfect for a quick and indulgent lunch.

Servings: 4
Preparation Time: 10 minutes
Cooking Time: 20 minutes
Ingredients:

- 2 lbs chicken wings, split and tips removed (900 g)
- 2 tablespoons olive oil (30 ml)
- 1 teaspoon garlic powder (5 g)
- 1/2 teaspoon paprika (2.5 g)
- Salt and pepper to taste
- 1/4 cup grated Parmesan cheese (30 g)
- 2 tablespoons chopped fresh parsley (optional, 10 g)

Directions:

1. Preheat the Ninja Foodi to 400°F (200°C).
2. Toss the chicken wings with olive oil, garlic powder, paprika, salt, and pepper. Place in one

basket and air fry for 18-20 minutes until crispy, shaking halfway through.

3. Remove the wings and toss with grated Parmesan cheese.
4. Garnish with chopped parsley if desired and serve hot.

20. Spaghetti Squash with Pesto and Cherry Tomatoes

A light and flavorful dish featuring spaghetti squash strands tossed with pesto and topped with fresh cherry tomatoes.

Servings: 4
Preparation Time: 10 minutes
Cooking Time: 25 minutes
Ingredients:

- 1 medium spaghetti squash, halved and seeds removed
- 2 tablespoons olive oil (30 ml)
- Salt and pepper to taste
- 1/2 cup pesto sauce (120 ml)
- 1 cup cherry tomatoes, halved (150 g)
- 1/4 cup grated Parmesan cheese (30 g)

Directions:

1. Preheat the Ninja Foodi to 375°F (190°C).
2. Drizzle the cut sides of the spaghetti squash with olive oil and season with salt and pepper. Place the squash halves in one basket, cut side down, and air fry for 20-25 minutes until tender.
3. Once cooked, use a fork to scrape out the squash into spaghetti-like strands.
4. Toss the spaghetti squash with pesto sauce and top with cherry tomatoes and grated Parmesan cheese. Serve warm.

Chapter 8: Family-Friendly Dinners

Dinner time is an important opportunity to gather with your family and enjoy a meal together. With the Ninja Foodi 2-Basket Air Fryer, you can prepare family-friendly dinners that are both delicious and nutritious, with minimal effort. Whether you're cooking for picky eaters or adventurous palates, these recipes will satisfy everyone at the table. From classic comfort foods to exciting new flavors, these dishes are perfect for busy weeknights or relaxed weekend dinners.

1. Crispy Chicken Tenders with Sweet Potato Fries

Tender chicken strips coated in a crunchy breadcrumb crust, paired with sweet potato fries—this is a kid-friendly dinner that the whole family will love.

Servings: 4
Preparation Time: 15 minutes
Cooking Time: 20 minutes
Ingredients:

- 1.5 lbs chicken tenders (680 g)
- 1 cup breadcrumbs (120 g)
- 1/2 cup grated Parmesan cheese (60 g)
- 1 teaspoon garlic powder (5 g)
- 1/2 teaspoon paprika (2.5 g)
- Salt and pepper to taste
- 2 large sweet potatoes, cut into fries
- 2 tablespoons olive oil (30 ml)

Directions:

1. Preheat the Ninja Foodi to 375°F (190°C).
2. In a shallow dish, combine breadcrumbs, Parmesan cheese, garlic powder, paprika, salt, and pepper.
3. Coat each chicken tender in the breadcrumb mixture, pressing to adhere.
4. In one basket, place the chicken tenders and air fry for 15-18 minutes, turning halfway through until golden and cooked through.
5. Toss the sweet potato fries with olive oil, salt, and pepper. Place in the second basket and air fry for 18-20 minutes, shaking halfway through until crispy.
6. Serve the chicken tenders with sweet potato fries and your favorite dipping sauces.

2. BBQ Meatloaf with Roasted Vegetables

A classic meatloaf with a tangy BBQ glaze, served with a side of perfectly roasted vegetables. This comforting dinner is sure to become a family favorite.

Servings: 4
Preparation Time: 15 minutes
Cooking Time: 25 minutes
Ingredients:

- 1 lb ground beef (450 g)
- 1/2 cup breadcrumbs (60 g)
- 1/4 cup milk (60 ml)
- 1 egg
- 1/2 onion, finely chopped
- 1 teaspoon dried thyme (5 g)
- Salt and pepper to taste
- 1/2 cup BBQ sauce (120 ml)
- 2 cups mixed vegetables (e.g., carrots, bell peppers, zucchini), chopped
- 2 tablespoons olive oil (30 ml)

Directions:

1. Preheat the Ninja Foodi to 375°F (190°C).

2. In a large bowl, combine ground beef, breadcrumbs, milk, egg, onion, thyme, salt, and pepper. Mix until well combined.
3. Shape the mixture into a loaf and place it in one basket. Brush with half of the BBQ sauce and air fry for 20-25 minutes, brushing with remaining BBQ sauce halfway through.
4. Toss the chopped vegetables with olive oil, salt, and pepper. Place in the second basket and air fry for 18-20 minutes until tender.
5. Serve the meatloaf with roasted vegetables.

3. Baked Ziti with Garlic Bread

This cheesy baked ziti is a comforting Italian classic, served with crispy garlic bread for a complete family meal.

Servings: 4
Preparation Time: 10 minutes
Cooking Time: 25 minutes
Ingredients:

- 8 oz ziti pasta (225 g)
- 2 cups marinara sauce (480 ml)
- 1 cup ricotta cheese (240 g)
- 1 cup shredded mozzarella cheese (120 g)
- 1/4 cup grated Parmesan cheese (30 g)
- 4 slices of Italian bread
- 2 tablespoons butter (30 g)
- 2 cloves garlic, minced
- 1 teaspoon dried oregano (5 g)

Directions:

1. Cook the ziti pasta according to package instructions until al dente. Drain and set aside.
2. Preheat the Ninja Foodi to 375°F (190°C).
3. In a mixing bowl, combine the cooked pasta, marinara sauce, ricotta cheese, half of the mozzarella, and half of the Parmesan. Mix well.
4. Transfer the pasta mixture to an air fryer-safe baking dish. Sprinkle the remaining mozzarella and Parmesan on top. Air fry in one basket for 20-25 minutes until the cheese is bubbly and golden.
5. In the second basket, place the Italian bread slices. Mix melted butter with minced garlic and oregano, then brush over the bread. Air fry at 350°F (175°C) for 5-7 minutes until crispy.

6. Serve the baked ziti with garlic bread.

4. Honey Garlic Glazed Salmon with Asparagus

A healthy and flavorful dinner featuring tender salmon fillets glazed with a sweet and savory honey garlic sauce, paired with roasted asparagus.

Servings: 4
Preparation Time: 10 minutes
Cooking Time: 15 minutes
Ingredients:

- 4 salmon fillets (about 6 oz each, 170 g)
- 2 tablespoons honey (30 ml)
- 2 tablespoons soy sauce (30 ml)
- 2 cloves garlic, minced
- 1 tablespoon olive oil (15 ml)
- 1 bunch asparagus, trimmed
- Salt and pepper to taste

Directions:

1. Preheat the Ninja Foodi to 375°F (190°C).
2. In a small bowl, whisk together honey, soy sauce, garlic, and olive oil.
3. Brush the salmon fillets with the honey garlic glaze and place them in one basket. Air fry for 10-12 minutes until the salmon is cooked through and slightly caramelized.
4. Toss the asparagus with olive oil, salt, and pepper. Place in the second basket and air fry for 10-12 minutes until tender.
5. Serve the salmon with roasted asparagus.

5. Cheesy Stuffed Peppers

Colorful bell peppers stuffed with a hearty mixture of ground beef, rice, and melted cheese, making for a satisfying and nutritious dinner.

Servings: 4
Preparation Time: 15 minutes
Cooking Time: 20 minutes
Ingredients:

- 4 large bell peppers, tops cut off and seeds removed
- 1 lb ground beef (450 g)
- 1 cup cooked rice (200 g)
- 1/2 onion, finely chopped

- 1 cup marinara sauce (240 ml)
- 1 cup shredded cheddar cheese (120 g)
- 1 teaspoon dried oregano (5 g)
- Salt and pepper to taste

Directions:
1. Preheat the Ninja Foodi to 375°F (190°C).
2. In a skillet, cook the ground beef and onion over medium heat until the beef is browned. Drain excess fat.
3. Stir in cooked rice, marinara sauce, oregano, salt, and pepper. Simmer for a few minutes until heated through.
4. Stuff each bell pepper with the beef and rice mixture. Top with shredded cheddar cheese.
5. Place the stuffed peppers in one basket and air fry for 15-20 minutes until the peppers are tender and the cheese is melted.
6. Serve hot and enjoy.

6. Teriyaki Chicken with Broccoli and Rice

Tender chicken thighs coated in a sweet and savory teriyaki sauce, served with steamed broccoli and rice for a balanced family dinner.

Servings: 4
Preparation Time: 10 minutes
Cooking Time: 20 minutes
Ingredients:
- 1.5 lbs boneless, skinless chicken thighs (680 g)
- 1/2 cup teriyaki sauce (120 ml)
- 4 cups cooked jasmine rice (800 g)
- 2 cups broccoli florets (300 g)
- 1 tablespoon sesame seeds (optional, 15 g)

Directions:
1. Preheat the Ninja Foodi to 375°F (190°C).
2. Toss the chicken thighs in the teriyaki sauce and place them in one basket. Air fry for 18-20 minutes until the chicken is fully cooked and glazed.
3. In the second basket, air fry the broccoli florets at 375°F (190°C) for 10-12 minutes until tender.
4. Serve the teriyaki chicken over jasmine rice, with a side of broccoli. Sprinkle with sesame seeds if desired.

7. Spaghetti and Meatballs

A classic Italian dinner featuring tender meatballs simmered in marinara sauce, served over spaghetti for a comforting family meal.

Servings: 4
Preparation Time: 15 minutes
Cooking Time: 20 minutes
Ingredients:
- 1 lb ground beef (450 g)
- 1/4 cup breadcrumbs (30 g)
- 1/4 cup grated Parmesan cheese (30 g)
- 1 egg
- 1 teaspoon dried basil (5 g)
- 1/2 teaspoon garlic powder (2.5 g)
- Salt and pepper to taste
- 2 cups marinara sauce (480 ml)
- 8 oz spaghetti (225 g), cooked according to package instructions

Directions:
1. Preheat the Ninja Foodi to 375°F (190°C).
2. In a bowl, combine ground beef, breadcrumbs, Parmesan cheese, egg, basil, garlic powder, salt, and pepper. Mix well and form into 12 meatballs.
3. Place the meatballs in one basket and air fry for 12-15 minutes until browned and cooked through.
4. Warm the marinara sauce in a saucepan over medium heat. Add the cooked meatballs to the sauce and simmer for a few minutes.
5. Serve the meatballs and sauce over cooked spaghetti, with extra Parmesan cheese if desired.

8. Chicken Parmesan with Garlic Bread

Crispy breaded chicken topped with marinara sauce and melted mozzarella, served with a side of garlic bread for a delicious Italian-inspired dinner.

Servings: 4
Preparation Time: 15 minutes
Cooking Time: 20 minutes
Ingredients:
- 1.5 lbs boneless, skinless chicken breasts (680 g)
- 1 cup breadcrumbs (120 g)
- 1/2 cup grated Parmesan cheese (60 g)
- 1 teaspoon dried oregano (5 g)

- 1 egg, beaten
- 1 cup marinara sauce (240 ml)
- 1 cup shredded mozzarella cheese (120 g)
- 4 slices of Italian bread
- 2 tablespoons butter (30 g)
- 2 cloves garlic, minced

Directions:
1. Preheat the Ninja Foodi to 375°F (190°C).
2. In a shallow dish, combine breadcrumbs, Parmesan cheese, and oregano.
3. Dip each chicken breast in beaten egg, then coat with the breadcrumb mixture.
4. Place the breaded chicken in one basket and air fry for 15-18 minutes until golden and cooked through.
5. Top each chicken breast with marinara sauce and shredded mozzarella cheese. Air fry for an additional 3-4 minutes until the cheese is melted.
6. In the second basket, place the Italian bread slices. Mix melted butter with minced garlic and spread over the bread. Air fry at 350°F (175°C) for 5-7 minutes until crispy.
7. Serve the Chicken Parmesan with garlic bread.

9. Beef and Vegetable Stir-Fry

Tender strips of beef stir-fried with colorful vegetables in a savory sauce, served over rice for a quick and satisfying family dinner.
Servings: 4
Preparation Time: 10 minutes
Cooking Time: 15 minutes
Ingredients:
- 1 lb beef sirloin, thinly sliced (450 g)
- 2 tablespoons soy sauce (30 ml)
- 1 tablespoon sesame oil (15 ml)
- 1 tablespoon honey (15 ml)
- 1 red bell pepper, sliced
- 1 zucchini, sliced
- 1 cup broccoli florets (150 g)
- 4 cups cooked rice (800 g)

Directions:
1. Preheat the Ninja Foodi to 375°F (190°C).
2. In a bowl, toss the beef slices with soy sauce, sesame oil, and honey. Place in one basket and

air fry for 10-12 minutes until the beef is browned.
3. In the second basket, air fry the bell pepper, zucchini, and broccoli at 375°F (190°C) for 8-10 minutes until tender.
4. Combine the cooked beef and vegetables in a bowl. Serve over cooked rice and enjoy.

10. Taco Night with All the Fixings

A fun and interactive dinner where everyone can build their own tacos with seasoned ground beef, fresh toppings, and warm tortillas.
Servings: 4
Preparation Time: 10 minutes
Cooking Time: 15 minutes
Ingredients:
- 1 lb ground beef (450 g)
- 1 tablespoon olive oil (15 ml)
- 1 packet taco seasoning (or homemade seasoning mix)
- 8 small corn or flour tortillas
- 1 cup shredded lettuce (50 g)
- 1 cup diced tomatoes (150 g)
- 1/2 cup shredded cheddar cheese (60 g)
- 1/4 cup sour cream (60 ml)
- 1/4 cup salsa (60 ml)

Directions:
1. Preheat the Ninja Foodi to 375°F (190°C).
2. In a skillet, heat olive oil over medium heat. Add ground beef and cook until browned. Stir in taco seasoning and a splash of water. Simmer for a few minutes until well combined.
3. Warm the tortillas in one basket at 350°F (175°C) for 2-3 minutes.
4. Set up a taco bar with seasoned beef, warm tortillas, lettuce, tomatoes, cheese, sour cream, and salsa.
5. Let everyone build their own tacos and enjoy a fun family meal.

11. Lemon Herb Roasted Chicken with Vegetables

A classic roasted chicken dinner flavored with lemon and herbs, served with a medley of roasted vegetables for a comforting family meal.

Servings: 4
Preparation Time: 15 minutes
Cooking Time: 40 minutes
Ingredients:

- 1 whole chicken (about 4 lbs, 1.8 kg)
- 2 lemons, halved
- 4 cloves garlic, minced
- 2 tablespoons olive oil (30 ml)
- 1 tablespoon dried thyme (15 g)
- 1 tablespoon dried rosemary (15 g)
- Salt and pepper to taste
- 4 large carrots, chopped
- 2 large potatoes, diced
- 1 onion, quartered

Directions:

1. Preheat the Ninja Foodi to 375°F (190°C).
2. In a small bowl, mix olive oil, garlic, thyme, rosemary, salt, and pepper. Rub the mixture all over the chicken, including under the skin.
3. Stuff the cavity of the chicken with lemon halves and place it in one basket.
4. Toss the chopped carrots, potatoes, and onion with olive oil, salt, and pepper. Place the vegetables in the second basket.
5. Air fry the chicken for 35-40 minutes, turning halfway through, until the internal temperature reaches 165°F (74°C).
6. Roast the vegetables for 30-35 minutes until tender and caramelized.
7. Let the chicken rest for 10 minutes before carving. Serve with the roasted vegetables.

12. Creamy Tuscan Chicken Pasta

Tender chicken in a creamy garlic sauce with sun-dried tomatoes and spinach, served over pasta for a rich and satisfying dinner.

Servings: 4
Preparation Time: 10 minutes
Cooking Time: 20 minutes
Ingredients:

- 1 lb boneless, skinless chicken breasts (450 g), sliced
- 2 tablespoons olive oil (30 ml)
- 2 cloves garlic, minced
- 1/2 cup sun-dried tomatoes, chopped (75 g)
- 1 cup heavy cream (240 ml)
- 1/2 cup grated Parmesan cheese (60 g)
- 2 cups baby spinach (60 g)
- 8 oz fettuccine or penne pasta (225 g), cooked according to package instructions
- Salt and pepper to taste

Directions:

1. Preheat the Ninja Foodi to 375°F (190°C).
2. Toss the chicken slices with olive oil, salt, and pepper. Place in one basket and air fry for 12-15 minutes until fully cooked.
3. In a large skillet, sauté garlic over medium heat until fragrant. Add sun-dried tomatoes, heavy cream, and Parmesan cheese. Simmer until the sauce thickens.
4. Stir in the cooked chicken and baby spinach, cooking until the spinach wilts.
5. Serve the creamy chicken sauce over the cooked pasta.

13. Beef Stroganoff with Egg Noodles

A rich and creamy beef stroganoff served over tender egg noodles for a comforting and hearty dinner.

Servings: 4
Preparation Time: 15 minutes
Cooking Time: 25 minutes
Ingredients:

- 1 lb beef sirloin, thinly sliced (450 g)
- 1 tablespoon olive oil (15 ml)
- 1 onion, finely chopped
- 2 cloves garlic, minced
- 1 cup mushrooms, sliced (150 g)
- 1 cup beef broth (240 ml)
- 1 cup sour cream (240 ml)
- 1 tablespoon Dijon mustard (15 g)
- 8 oz egg noodles (225 g), cooked according to package instructions
- Salt and pepper to taste

Directions:
1. Preheat the Ninja Foodi to 375°F (190°C).
2. Toss the beef slices with olive oil, salt, and pepper. Place in one basket and air fry for 10-12 minutes until browned.
3. In a large skillet, sauté onion and garlic over medium heat until softened. Add mushrooms and cook until tender.
4. Stir in beef broth, sour cream, and Dijon mustard. Simmer until the sauce thickens slightly.
5. Add the cooked beef to the sauce and serve over egg noodles.

14. Baked Lemon Garlic Shrimp with Rice

Juicy shrimp baked in a lemon garlic butter sauce, served over rice for a quick and flavorful dinner.
Servings: 4
Preparation Time: 10 minutes
Cooking Time: 15 minutes
Ingredients:
- 1.5 lbs large shrimp, peeled and deveined (680 g)
- 3 cloves garlic, minced
- 1/4 cup butter, melted (60 g)
- 2 tablespoons lemon juice (30 ml)
- 1 teaspoon paprika (5 g)
- Salt and pepper to taste
- 4 cups cooked jasmine rice (800 g)
- 2 tablespoons fresh parsley, chopped (optional, 10 g)

Directions:
1. Preheat the Ninja Foodi to 375°F (190°C).
2. In a bowl, combine melted butter, garlic, lemon juice, paprika, salt, and pepper. Toss the shrimp in the mixture.
3. Place the shrimp in one basket and air fry for 10-12 minutes until pink and cooked through.
4. Serve the shrimp over cooked jasmine rice and garnish with chopped parsley if desired.

15. Stuffed Pork Chops with Apples and Onions

Pork chops stuffed with a savory apple and onion mixture, then baked to juicy perfection for a cozy fall-inspired dinner.
Servings: 4
Preparation Time: 15 minutes
Cooking Time: 25 minutes
Ingredients:
- 4 thick-cut pork chops
- 1 apple, peeled and diced
- 1 small onion, finely chopped
- 1/4 cup breadcrumbs (30 g)
- 2 tablespoons butter (30 g)
- 1 teaspoon dried sage (5 g)
- Salt and pepper to taste

Directions:
1. Preheat the Ninja Foodi to 375°F (190°C).
2. In a skillet, melt butter over medium heat. Add diced apple, onion, and dried sage. Cook until softened. Stir in breadcrumbs and season with salt and pepper.
3. Cut a pocket into each pork chop and stuff with the apple mixture.
4. Place the stuffed pork chops in one basket and air fry for 20-25 minutes until the internal temperature reaches 145°F (63°C).
5. Let the pork chops rest for 5 minutes before serving.

16. Veggie Lasagna

Layers of tender pasta, rich marinara sauce, and a blend of vegetables and cheeses make this a hearty and satisfying vegetarian dinner.
Servings: 4
Preparation Time: 20 minutes
Cooking Time: 25 minutes
Ingredients:
- 8 oz lasagna noodles (225 g), cooked according to package instructions
- 2 cups marinara sauce (480 ml)
- 1 cup ricotta cheese (240 g)
- 1 cup shredded mozzarella cheese (120 g)
- 1/4 cup grated Parmesan cheese (30 g)
- 1 zucchini, thinly sliced

- 1 cup mushrooms, sliced (150 g)
- 1/2 cup spinach (30 g)
- Salt and pepper to taste

Directions:
1. Preheat the Ninja Foodi to 375°F (190°C).
2. In a baking dish, spread a thin layer of marinara sauce. Layer with cooked lasagna noodles, ricotta cheese, zucchini slices, mushrooms, spinach, and mozzarella cheese. Repeat layers, ending with a layer of noodles and sauce.
3. Top with Parmesan cheese.
4. Place the lasagna in one basket and air fry for 20-25 minutes until the cheese is bubbly and golden.
5. Let the lasagna rest for 5 minutes before slicing and serving.

17. Chicken Fajitas

Juicy chicken strips with bell peppers and onions, all seasoned with classic fajita spices and served with warm tortillas for a fun and interactive family dinner.

Servings: 4
Preparation Time: 10 minutes
Cooking Time: 15 minutes
Ingredients:
- 1.5 lbs boneless, skinless chicken breasts, sliced (680 g)
- 1 red bell pepper, sliced
- 1 green bell pepper, sliced
- 1 onion, sliced
- 2 tablespoons olive oil (30 ml)
- 1 teaspoon chili powder (5 g)
- 1 teaspoon cumin (5 g)
- 1/2 teaspoon garlic powder (2.5 g)
- Salt and pepper to taste
- 8 small flour tortillas

Directions:
1. Preheat the Ninja Foodi to 375°F (190°C).
2. In a bowl, toss chicken strips, bell peppers, and onion with olive oil, chili powder, cumin, garlic powder, salt, and pepper.
3. Place the mixture in one basket and air fry for 12-15 minutes until the chicken is cooked through and the vegetables are tender.

4. Warm the tortillas in the second basket at 350°F (175°C) for 1-2 minutes.
5. Serve the chicken fajitas with warm tortillas and your favorite toppings like salsa, sour cream, and guacamole.

18. Maple Dijon Glazed Pork Tenderloin with Green Beans

A tender pork tenderloin glazed with a sweet and tangy maple Dijon sauce, served with crisp green beans for a balanced and flavorful dinner.

Servings: 4
Preparation Time: 10 minutes
Cooking Time: 25 minutes
Ingredients:
- 1.5 lbs pork tenderloin (680 g)
- 1/4 cup maple syrup (60 ml)
- 2 tablespoons Dijon mustard (30 g)
- 1 tablespoon olive oil (15 ml)
- 1 lb green beans, trimmed (450 g)
- Salt and pepper to taste

Directions:
1. Preheat the Ninja Foodi to 375°F (190°C).
2. In a small bowl, whisk together maple syrup, Dijon mustard, olive oil, salt, and pepper. Brush the glaze over the pork tenderloin.
3. Place the pork tenderloin in one basket and air fry for 20-25 minutes until the internal temperature reaches 145°F (63°C), brushing with glaze halfway through.
4. Toss the green beans with olive oil, salt, and pepper. Place in the second basket and air fry for 12-15 minutes until tender.
5. Let the pork tenderloin rest for 5 minutes before slicing. Serve with green beans.

19. Chili-Lime Shrimp with Mexican Rice

Spicy shrimp seasoned with chili and lime, served over flavorful Mexican rice for a zesty and vibrant dinner.

Servings: 4
Preparation Time: 10 minutes
Cooking Time: 15 minutes
Ingredients:

- 1.5 lbs large shrimp, peeled and deveined (680 g)
- 2 tablespoons olive oil (30 ml)
- 1 teaspoon chili powder (5 g)
- 1/2 teaspoon cumin (2.5 g)
- Juice of 1 lime
- Salt and pepper to taste
- 4 cups cooked Mexican rice (800 g)
- 1/4 cup chopped cilantro (optional, 15 g)

Directions:

1. Preheat the Ninja Foodi to 375°F (190°C).
2. Toss the shrimp with olive oil, chili powder, cumin, lime juice, salt, and pepper.
3. Place the shrimp in one basket and air fry for 8-10 minutes until pink and cooked through.
4. Serve the shrimp over Mexican rice and garnish with chopped cilantro if desired.

20. BBQ Pulled Chicken Sandwiches

Tender shredded chicken coated in a tangy BBQ sauce, served on toasted buns with a side of coleslaw for a fun and easy family dinner.

Servings: 4
Preparation Time: 10 minutes
Cooking Time: 20 minutes
Ingredients:

- 1.5 lbs boneless, skinless chicken breasts (680 g)
- 1 cup BBQ sauce (240 ml)
- 4 sandwich buns
- 1/2 cup coleslaw (optional, 60 g)

Directions:

1. Preheat the Ninja Foodi to 375°F (190°C).
2. Place the chicken breasts in one basket and air fry for 15-18 minutes until fully cooked.
3. Shred the chicken with two forks and toss with BBQ sauce.
4. Toast the sandwich buns in the second basket at 350°F (175°C) for 2-3 minutes.
5. Assemble the sandwiches by piling the BBQ pulled chicken onto the buns and topping with coleslaw if desired. Serve immediately.

Chapter 9: Sides and Veggies

No meal is complete without delicious sides and veggies to complement your main dishes. With the Ninja Foodi 2-Basket Air Fryer, you can create healthy and tasty side dishes with ease. From crispy potatoes to flavorful roasted vegetables, these recipes are designed to enhance your meals without taking up too much time. Whether you're looking for something simple or a bit more adventurous, these ten recipes will add variety and nutrition to your family dinners.

1. Crispy Parmesan Brussels Sprouts

These Brussels sprouts are roasted to crispy perfection and topped with Parmesan cheese, making them a delicious and nutritious side dish.

Servings: 4
Preparation Time: 10 minutes
Cooking Time: 15 minutes
Ingredients:

- 1 lb Brussels sprouts, trimmed and halved (450 g)
- 2 tablespoons olive oil (30 ml)
- 1/4 cup grated Parmesan cheese (30 g)
- 1 teaspoon garlic powder (5 g)
- Salt and pepper to taste

Directions:

1. Preheat the Ninja Foodi to 375°F (190°C).
2. In a large bowl, toss the Brussels sprouts with olive oil, garlic powder, salt, and pepper.
3. Place the Brussels sprouts in one basket and air fry for 12-15 minutes until crispy and golden, shaking the basket halfway through.
4. Sprinkle with Parmesan cheese and serve immediately.

2. Garlic Herb Roasted Potatoes

These roasted potatoes are crispy on the outside and tender on the inside, seasoned with a blend of garlic and herbs.

Servings: 4
Preparation Time: 10 minutes
Cooking Time: 20 minutes
Ingredients:

- 1.5 lbs baby potatoes, halved (680 g)
- 2 tablespoons olive oil (30 ml)
- 3 cloves garlic, minced
- 1 teaspoon dried rosemary (5 g)
- 1 teaspoon dried thyme (5 g)
- Salt and pepper to taste

Directions:

1. Preheat the Ninja Foodi to 400°F (200°C).
2. In a bowl, toss the potatoes with olive oil, garlic, rosemary, thyme, salt, and pepper.
3. Place the potatoes in one basket and air fry for 18-20 minutes until crispy, shaking the basket halfway through.
4. Serve hot and enjoy as a side to your favorite main dish.

3. Roasted Carrots with Honey and Balsamic

Sweet and tangy, these roasted carrots are glazed with honey and balsamic vinegar, making them a perfect accompaniment to any meal.

Servings: 4
Preparation Time: 10 minutes
Cooking Time: 20 minutes
Ingredients:

- 1 lb carrots, peeled and cut into sticks (450 g)
- 2 tablespoons olive oil (30 ml)
- 1 tablespoon honey (15 ml)
- 1 tablespoon balsamic vinegar (15 ml)
- Salt and pepper to taste

Directions:

1. Preheat the Ninja Foodi to 375°F (190°C).
2. Toss the carrots with olive oil, honey, balsamic vinegar, salt, and pepper in a large bowl.
3. Place the carrots in one basket and air fry for 18-20 minutes until tender and caramelized, shaking the basket halfway through.
4. Serve as a sweet and savory side dish.

4. Smashed Potatoes with Garlic Butter

These crispy smashed potatoes are brushed with garlic butter and roasted until golden brown, making them a delicious and satisfying side.

Servings: 4
Preparation Time: 15 minutes
Cooking Time: 25 minutes
Ingredients:

- 1.5 lbs baby potatoes (680 g)
- 3 tablespoons butter, melted (45 g)
- 2 cloves garlic, minced
- 1 teaspoon dried parsley (5 g)
- Salt and pepper to taste

Directions:

1. Preheat the Ninja Foodi to 400°F (200°C).
2. Boil the potatoes in salted water for 10 minutes until tender. Drain and let cool slightly.
3. Place the potatoes on a cutting board and gently smash them with the bottom of a glass.
4. In a small bowl, mix melted butter, garlic, parsley, salt, and pepper.
5. Place the smashed potatoes in one basket, brush with garlic butter, and air fry for 20-25 minutes until crispy.
6. Serve hot and enjoy.

5. Lemon Garlic Asparagus

This simple and flavorful asparagus is roasted with lemon and garlic, making it a quick and healthy side dish.

Servings: 4
Preparation Time: 5 minutes
Cooking Time: 10 minutes
Ingredients:

- 1 bunch asparagus, trimmed (about 1 lb, 450 g)
- 1 tablespoon olive oil (15 ml)
- 2 cloves garlic, minced
- Juice of 1 lemon
- Salt and pepper to taste

Directions:

1. Preheat the Ninja Foodi to 375°F (190°C).
2. Toss the asparagus with olive oil, garlic, lemon juice, salt, and pepper in a bowl.
3. Place the asparagus in one basket and air fry for 8-10 minutes until tender-crisp.
4. Serve immediately as a light and refreshing side dish.

6. Sweet and Spicy Roasted Cauliflower

This cauliflower is roasted with a sweet and spicy glaze, creating a flavorful side dish with a bit of a kick.

Servings: 4
Preparation Time: 10 minutes
Cooking Time: 20 minutes
Ingredients:

- 1 head cauliflower, cut into florets
- 2 tablespoons olive oil (30 ml)
- 1 tablespoon honey (15 ml)
- 1 teaspoon smoked paprika (5 g)
- 1/2 teaspoon cayenne pepper (2.5 g)
- Salt and pepper to taste

Directions:

1. Preheat the Ninja Foodi to 375°F (190°C).
2. In a large bowl, toss the cauliflower florets with olive oil, honey, smoked paprika, cayenne pepper, salt, and pepper.

3. Place the cauliflower in one basket and air fry for 18-20 minutes until caramelized and tender, shaking the basket halfway through.
4. Serve hot as a bold and flavorful side.

7. Herb-Crusted Zucchini Fries

These crispy zucchini fries are coated in herbs and breadcrumbs, making them a healthier alternative to traditional fries.

Servings: 4
Preparation Time: 10 minutes
Cooking Time: 15 minutes
Ingredients:

- 2 large zucchinis, cut into fries
- 1 cup breadcrumbs (120 g)
- 1/4 cup grated Parmesan cheese (30 g)
- 1 teaspoon dried oregano (5 g)
- 1 teaspoon dried basil (5 g)
- 1/2 teaspoon garlic powder (2.5 g)
- Salt and pepper to taste
- 2 eggs, beaten

Directions:

1. Preheat the Ninja Foodi to 400°F (200°C).
2. In a shallow dish, mix breadcrumbs, Parmesan cheese, oregano, basil, garlic powder, salt, and pepper.
3. Dip the zucchini fries into the beaten eggs, then coat with the breadcrumb mixture.
4. Place the zucchini fries in one basket and air fry for 12-15 minutes until golden and crispy, shaking the basket halfway through.
5. Serve with your favorite dipping sauce.

8. Cheesy Broccoli Casserole

This comforting broccoli casserole is baked with a cheesy sauce, making it a perfect side dish for any family meal.

Servings: 4
Preparation Time: 10 minutes
Cooking Time: 20 minutes
Ingredients:

- 1 lb broccoli florets (450 g)
- 1 cup shredded cheddar cheese (120 g)
- 1/4 cup sour cream (60 ml)
- 1/4 cup mayonnaise (60 ml)

- 1/2 teaspoon garlic powder (2.5 g)
- Salt and pepper to taste
- 1/4 cup breadcrumbs (30 g)

Directions:

1. Preheat the Ninja Foodi to 375°F (190°C).
2. In a large bowl, mix together cheddar cheese, sour cream, mayonnaise, garlic powder, salt, and pepper.
3. Toss the broccoli florets with the cheese mixture until well coated.
4. Transfer the mixture to an air fryer-safe baking dish and sprinkle with breadcrumbs.
5. Place the dish in one basket and air fry for 18-20 minutes until the top is golden and bubbly.
6. Serve hot as a cheesy and delicious side dish.

9. Maple-Glazed Carrots

These roasted carrots are glazed with maple syrup and butter, creating a sweet and savory side dish that pairs well with any meal.

Servings: 4
Preparation Time: 10 minutes
Cooking Time: 15 minutes
Ingredients:

- 1 lb carrots, peeled and sliced (450 g)
- 2 tablespoons butter, melted (30 g)
- 2 tablespoons maple syrup (30 ml)
- Salt and pepper to taste

Directions:

1. Preheat the Ninja Foodi to 375°F (190°C).
2. In a large bowl, toss the carrots with melted butter, maple syrup, salt, and pepper.
3. Place the carrots in one basket and air fry for 15-18 minutes until tender and caramelized, shaking the basket halfway through.
4. Serve as a sweet and savory side dish.

10. Spicy Garlic Green Beans

These green beans are sautéed with garlic and a touch of red pepper flakes, creating a flavorful and slightly spicy side dish.

Servings: 4
Preparation Time: 5 minutes
Cooking Time: 10 minutes

Ingredients:
- 1 lb green beans, trimmed (450 g)
- 1 tablespoon olive oil (15 ml)
- 3 cloves garlic, minced
- 1/2 teaspoon red pepper flakes (2.5 g)
- Salt and pepper to taste

Directions:
1. Preheat the Ninja Foodi to 375°F (190°C).
2. Toss the green beans with olive oil, garlic, red pepper flakes, salt, and pepper in a large bowl.
3. Place the green beans in one basket and air fry for 8-10 minutes until tender-crisp.
4. Serve hot as a flavorful and slightly spicy side dish.

11. Crispy Baked Kale Chips

Light and crispy kale chips seasoned with a touch of sea salt and garlic, making for a healthy and addictive snack or side.

Servings: 4
Preparation Time: 5 minutes
Cooking Time: 10 minutes
Ingredients:
- 1 large bunch kale, stems removed and torn into bite-sized pieces
- 1 tablespoon olive oil (15 ml)
- 1/2 teaspoon garlic powder (2.5 g)
- 1/2 teaspoon sea salt (2.5 g)

Directions:
1. Preheat the Ninja Foodi to 350°F (175°C).
2. In a large bowl, toss the kale pieces with olive oil, garlic powder, and sea salt until evenly coated.
3. Place the kale in one basket in a single layer and air fry for 8-10 minutes until crispy, shaking the basket halfway through.
4. Serve immediately for a light and crunchy snack or side.

12. Roasted Garlic Mashed Cauliflower

A creamy and garlicky mashed cauliflower that's a lower-carb alternative to mashed potatoes, but just as satisfying.

Servings: 4
Preparation Time: 10 minutes
Cooking Time: 15 minutes
Ingredients:
- 1 large head of cauliflower, cut into florets
- 4 cloves garlic, minced
- 2 tablespoons butter (30 g)
- 1/4 cup sour cream (60 ml)
- Salt and pepper to taste
- 1 tablespoon fresh chives, chopped (optional, 5 g)

Directions:
1. Preheat the Ninja Foodi to 375°F (190°C).
2. Place the cauliflower florets and garlic in one basket and air fry for 12-15 minutes until the cauliflower is tender.
3. Transfer the cauliflower and garlic to a food processor. Add butter, sour cream, salt, and pepper, and blend until smooth and creamy.
4. Serve hot, garnished with chopped chives if desired.

13. Herb-Roasted Root Vegetables

A mix of root vegetables roasted with fresh herbs for a flavorful and nutritious side dish.

Servings: 4
Preparation Time: 10 minutes
Cooking Time: 25 minutes
Ingredients:
- 2 carrots, sliced
- 2 parsnips, sliced
- 1 sweet potato, diced
- 1 small beet, diced
- 2 tablespoons olive oil (30 ml)
- 1 teaspoon dried thyme (5 g)
- 1 teaspoon dried rosemary (5 g)
- Salt and pepper to taste

Directions:
1. Preheat the Ninja Foodi to 375°F (190°C).
2. In a large bowl, toss the root vegetables with olive oil, thyme, rosemary, salt, and pepper.
3. Place the vegetables in one basket and air fry for 20-25 minutes until tender and caramelized, shaking the basket halfway through.
4. Serve as a hearty and flavorful side dish.

14. Balsamic Glazed Brussels Sprouts

These Brussels sprouts are roasted to perfection and finished with a sweet and tangy balsamic glaze.

Servings: 4
Preparation Time: 5 minutes
Cooking Time: 15 minutes
Ingredients:

- 1 lb Brussels sprouts, trimmed and halved (450 g)
- 2 tablespoons olive oil (30 ml)
- 1/4 cup balsamic vinegar (60 ml)
- 1 tablespoon honey (15 ml)
- Salt and pepper to taste

Directions:

1. Preheat the Ninja Foodi to 375°F (190°C).
2. Toss the Brussels sprouts with olive oil, salt, and pepper.
3. Place the Brussels sprouts in one basket and air fry for 12-15 minutes until crispy and golden.
4. Meanwhile, in a small saucepan, simmer balsamic vinegar and honey over medium heat until thickened, about 5 minutes.
5. Drizzle the balsamic glaze over the roasted Brussels sprouts before serving.

15. Spicy Sriracha Roasted Chickpeas

Crispy roasted chickpeas with a kick of Sriracha, perfect as a snack or crunchy salad topping.

Servings: 4
Preparation Time: 5 minutes
Cooking Time: 15 minutes
Ingredients:

- 1 can chickpeas, drained and rinsed (15 oz, 425 g)
- 1 tablespoon olive oil (15 ml)
- 1 tablespoon Sriracha sauce (15 ml)
- 1/2 teaspoon smoked paprika (2.5 g)
- Salt to taste

Directions:

1. Preheat the Ninja Foodi to 375°F (190°C).
2. In a bowl, toss the chickpeas with olive oil, Sriracha, smoked paprika, and salt.
3. Place the chickpeas in one basket and air fry for 12-15 minutes until crispy, shaking the basket halfway through.
4. Serve as a spicy snack or crunchy topping for salads and soups.

16. Maple-Roasted Butternut Squash

Tender butternut squash cubes roasted with maple syrup and cinnamon for a sweet and comforting side dish.

Servings: 4
Preparation Time: 10 minutes
Cooking Time: 20 minutes
Ingredients:

- 1 butternut squash, peeled and cubed
- 2 tablespoons maple syrup (30 ml)
- 1 tablespoon olive oil (15 ml)
- 1/2 teaspoon ground cinnamon (2.5 g)
- Salt to taste

Directions:

1. Preheat the Ninja Foodi to 375°F (190°C).
2. Toss the butternut squash cubes with maple syrup, olive oil, cinnamon, and salt.
3. Place the squash in one basket and air fry for 18-20 minutes until tender and caramelized, shaking the basket halfway through.
4. Serve hot as a sweet and savory side dish.

17. Parmesan Crusted Asparagus

Asparagus spears coated in Parmesan cheese and breadcrumbs, then roasted to crispy perfection.

Servings: 4
Preparation Time: 5 minutes
Cooking Time: 10 minutes
Ingredients:

- 1 bunch asparagus, trimmed (about 1 lb, 450 g)
- 1/4 cup grated Parmesan cheese (30 g)
- 1/4 cup breadcrumbs (30 g)
- 1 tablespoon olive oil (15 ml)
- Salt and pepper to taste

Directions:

1. Preheat the Ninja Foodi to 375°F (190°C).
2. Toss the asparagus with olive oil, salt, and pepper.
3. In a shallow dish, mix Parmesan cheese and breadcrumbs. Roll each asparagus spear in the mixture to coat.

4. Place the coated asparagus in one basket and air fry for 8-10 minutes until crispy.
5. Serve immediately as a crunchy and cheesy side dish.

18. Cajun Spiced Sweet Potato Wedges

Sweet potato wedges seasoned with bold Cajun spices and roasted until crispy, perfect for spicing up any meal.
Servings: 4
Preparation Time: 10 minutes
Cooking Time: 20 minutes
Ingredients:
- 2 large sweet potatoes, cut into wedges
- 2 tablespoons olive oil (30 ml)
- 1 tablespoon Cajun seasoning (15 g)
- 1/2 teaspoon garlic powder (2.5 g)
- Salt to taste

Directions:
1. Preheat the Ninja Foodi to 400°F (200°C).
2. In a large bowl, toss the sweet potato wedges with olive oil, Cajun seasoning, garlic powder, and salt.
3. Place the wedges in one basket and air fry for 18-20 minutes until crispy, shaking the basket halfway through.
4. Serve hot with your favorite dipping sauce.

19. Garlic Butter Mushrooms

Juicy mushrooms sautéed in garlic butter, perfect as a side dish or a topping for steak or chicken.
Servings: 4
Preparation Time: 5 minutes
Cooking Time: 10 minutes
Ingredients:
- 1 lb mushrooms, sliced (450 g)
- 2 tablespoons butter (30 g)
- 3 cloves garlic, minced
- 1 tablespoon fresh parsley, chopped (optional, 5 g)
- Salt and pepper to taste

Directions:
1. Preheat the Ninja Foodi to 375°F (190°C).
2. Melt the butter in a small saucepan and add the minced garlic. Cook until fragrant.
3. Toss the mushrooms with the garlic butter, salt, and pepper.
4. Place the mushrooms in one basket and air fry for 8-10 minutes until tender and golden.
5. Garnish with chopped parsley and serve hot.

20. Mediterranean Roasted Vegetables

A colorful mix of Mediterranean vegetables roasted with olive oil and herbs, perfect as a versatile side dish.
Servings: 4
Preparation Time: 10 minutes
Cooking Time: 20 minutes
Ingredients:
- 1 zucchini, sliced
- 1 eggplant, diced
- 1 red bell pepper, sliced
- 1 red onion, sliced
- 2 tablespoons olive oil (30 ml)
- 1 teaspoon dried oregano (5 g)
- 1 teaspoon dried thyme (5 g)
- Salt and pepper to taste

Directions:
1. Preheat the Ninja Foodi to 375°F (190°C).
2. In a large bowl, toss the zucchini, eggplant, bell pepper, and red onion with olive oil, oregano, thyme, salt, and pepper.
3. Place the vegetables in one basket and air fry for 18-20 minutes until tender and slightly charred, shaking the basket halfway through.
4. Serve hot as a versatile and flavorful side dish that pairs well with a variety of main courses.

Chapter 10: Appetizers and Snacks

Appetizers and snacks are perfect for setting the tone of a meal or satisfying mid-day cravings. With the Ninja Foodi 2-Basket Air Fryer, you can whip up these delicious bites quickly and easily. Whether you're hosting a party or just looking for a light snack, these recipes will impress your guests and keep everyone coming back for more. Here are ten recipes that are simple, healthy, and packed with flavor.

1. Crispy Coconut Shrimp

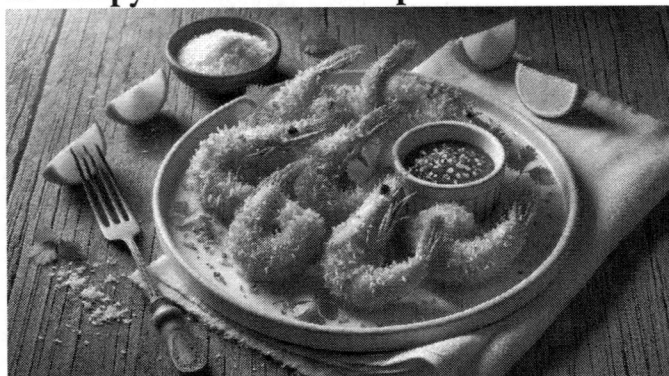

Golden and crunchy coconut shrimp that pair perfectly with sweet chili sauce, offering a delightful tropical twist.

Servings: 4
Preparation Time: 15 minutes
Cooking Time: 10 minutes
Ingredients:
- 1 lb large shrimp, peeled and deveined (450 g)
- 1/2 cup all-purpose flour (60 g)
- 2 eggs, beaten
- 1 cup shredded coconut (100 g)
- 1/2 cup panko breadcrumbs (60 g)
- 1/2 teaspoon salt (2.5 g)
- 1/4 teaspoon black pepper (1.5 g)
- Sweet chili sauce for dipping

Directions:
1. Preheat the Ninja Foodi to 375°F (190°C).
2. In three separate shallow bowls, place the flour, beaten eggs, and a mixture of shredded coconut, panko breadcrumbs, salt, and pepper.
3. Dredge each shrimp in flour, dip in the egg, and then coat with the coconut-panko mixture.
4. Place the shrimp in one basket in a single layer and air fry for 8-10 minutes until golden and crispy, flipping halfway through.
5. Serve hot with sweet chili sauce for dipping.

2. Loaded Potato Skins

Crispy potato skins loaded with melted cheese, crispy bacon, and green onions—an irresistible snack for any occasion.

Servings: 4
Preparation Time: 15 minutes
Cooking Time: 20 minutes
Ingredients:
- 4 medium russet potatoes
- 1 cup shredded cheddar cheese (120 g)
- 4 slices bacon, cooked and crumbled
- 2 green onions, sliced
- 2 tablespoons olive oil (30 ml)
- Salt and pepper to taste
- Sour cream for serving

Directions:
1. Preheat the Ninja Foodi to 400°F (200°C).
2. Pierce the potatoes with a fork and air fry in one basket for 35-40 minutes until tender. Let them cool slightly.
3. Cut the potatoes in half lengthwise and scoop out most of the flesh, leaving a thin layer inside the skins.
4. Brush the potato skins with olive oil, season with salt and pepper, and air fry for 5-7 minutes until crispy.

5. Fill the skins with cheddar cheese and crumbled bacon. Air fry for an additional 3-5 minutes until the cheese is melted.

6. Top with sliced green onions and serve with sour cream.

3. Garlic Parmesan Chicken Wings

Juicy chicken wings tossed in a savory garlic Parmesan sauce, perfect for game day or any casual gathering.

Servings: 4
Preparation Time: 10 minutes
Cooking Time: 20 minutes
Ingredients:

- 2 lbs chicken wings, split and tips removed (900 g)
- 2 tablespoons olive oil (30 ml)
- 1 teaspoon garlic powder (5 g)
- 1/2 teaspoon smoked paprika (2.5 g)
- 1/4 cup grated Parmesan cheese (30 g)
- 2 tablespoons fresh parsley, chopped (optional, 10 g)
- Salt and pepper to taste

Directions:

1. Preheat the Ninja Foodi to 400°F (200°C).
2. Toss the chicken wings with olive oil, garlic powder, smoked paprika, salt, and pepper.
3. Place the wings in one basket in a single layer and air fry for 18-20 minutes until crispy, shaking the basket halfway through.
4. Toss the hot wings with grated Parmesan cheese and chopped parsley if using.
5. Serve immediately.

4. Mozzarella Sticks

Crispy on the outside, gooey on the inside, these mozzarella sticks are a classic snack that everyone will love.

Servings: 4
Preparation Time: 15 minutes (plus 1 hour freezing time)
Cooking Time: 8 minutes
Ingredients:

- 12 mozzarella sticks
- 1/2 cup all-purpose flour (60 g)
- 2 eggs, beaten

- 1 cup panko breadcrumbs (120 g)
- 1 teaspoon Italian seasoning (5 g)
- 1/2 teaspoon garlic powder (2.5 g)
- Marinara sauce for dipping

Directions:

1. Cut the mozzarella sticks in half and freeze for at least 1 hour.
2. Preheat the Ninja Foodi to 400°F (200°C).
3. Set up a breading station with three shallow dishes: one with flour, one with beaten eggs, and one with panko breadcrumbs mixed with Italian seasoning and garlic powder.
4. Dredge each frozen mozzarella stick in flour, dip in the egg, and then coat with the breadcrumb mixture.
5. Place the mozzarella sticks in one basket and air fry for 6-8 minutes until golden and crispy, shaking the basket halfway through.
6. Serve with warm marinara sauce for dipping.

5. Spicy Buffalo Cauliflower Bites

These cauliflower bites are tossed in a spicy buffalo sauce, offering a healthier alternative to buffalo wings.

Servings: 4
Preparation Time: 10 minutes
Cooking Time: 15 minutes
Ingredients:

- 1 medium head cauliflower, cut into florets
- 1/2 cup all-purpose flour (60 g)
- 1/2 cup water (120 ml)
- 1 teaspoon garlic powder (5 g)
- 1/2 teaspoon smoked paprika (2.5 g)
- 1/2 cup buffalo sauce (120 ml)
- 2 tablespoons butter, melted (30 g)
- Salt and pepper to taste

Directions:

1. Preheat the Ninja Foodi to 375°F (190°C).
2. In a large bowl, whisk together flour, water, garlic powder, smoked paprika, salt, and pepper to create a batter.
3. Toss the cauliflower florets in the batter until evenly coated.
4. Place the cauliflower in one basket in a single layer and air fry for 12-15 minutes until crispy, shaking the basket halfway through.

5. In a small bowl, mix buffalo sauce with melted butter. Toss the hot cauliflower in the sauce.
6. Serve with celery sticks and blue cheese dressing.

6. Jalapeño Poppers

Creamy, cheesy jalapeño poppers with a crispy breadcrumb coating, perfect for spicing up your appetizer spread.

Servings: 4
Preparation Time: 15 minutes
Cooking Time: 10 minutes
Ingredients:
- 8 large jalapeños, halved and seeded
- 4 oz cream cheese, softened (115 g)
- 1/2 cup shredded cheddar cheese (60 g)
- 1/4 cup panko breadcrumbs (30 g)
- 1/4 cup cooked bacon, crumbled (optional, 30 g)
- 1 egg, beaten
- Salt and pepper to taste

Directions:
1. Preheat the Ninja Foodi to 375°F (190°C).
2. In a bowl, mix the cream cheese, cheddar cheese, crumbled bacon (if using), salt, and pepper.
3. Stuff each jalapeño half with the cheese mixture.
4. Dip the stuffed jalapeños in beaten egg, then coat with panko breadcrumbs.
5. Place the jalapeño poppers in one basket in a single layer and air fry for 8-10 minutes until the breadcrumbs are golden and crispy.
6. Serve hot.

7. Crispy Chickpeas

These roasted chickpeas are crunchy, flavorful, and highly addictive—perfect as a snack or salad topper.

Servings: 4
Preparation Time: 5 minutes
Cooking Time: 15 minutes
Ingredients:
- 1 can chickpeas, drained and rinsed (15 oz, 425 g)
- 1 tablespoon olive oil (15 ml)
- 1 teaspoon smoked paprika (5 g)
- 1/2 teaspoon garlic powder (2.5 g)
- 1/2 teaspoon cumin (2.5 g)
- Salt to taste

Directions:
1. Preheat the Ninja Foodi to 375°F (190°C).
2. In a bowl, toss the chickpeas with olive oil, smoked paprika, garlic powder, cumin, and salt.
3. Place the chickpeas in one basket in a single layer and air fry for 12-15 minutes until crispy, shaking the basket halfway through.
4. Serve as a snack or a crunchy addition to salads.

8. Spinach and Artichoke Dip

A warm, creamy spinach and artichoke dip that's perfect for dipping with chips, crackers, or veggies.

Servings: 4
Preparation Time: 10 minutes
Cooking Time: 10 minutes
Ingredients:
- 1 cup frozen spinach, thawed and drained (150 g)
- 1/2 cup marinated artichoke hearts, chopped (120 g)
- 1/2 cup cream cheese, softened (115 g)
- 1/4 cup sour cream (60 ml)
- 1/4 cup mayonnaise (60 ml)
- 1/2 cup shredded mozzarella cheese (60 g)
- 1/4 cup grated Parmesan cheese (30 g)
- 1 clove garlic, minced
- Salt and pepper to taste

Directions:
1. Preheat the Ninja Foodi to 375°F (190°C).
2. In a mixing bowl, combine spinach, artichoke hearts, cream cheese, sour cream, mayonnaise, mozzarella, Parmesan, garlic, salt, and pepper.
3. Transfer the mixture to an air fryer-safe dish and place it in one basket.
4. Air fry for 8-10 minutes until the dip is bubbly and golden on top.
5. Serve warm with chips, crackers, or fresh veggies.

9. Bacon-Wrapped Jalapeño Bites

Spicy jalapeños stuffed with cream cheese and wrapped in crispy bacon, a crowd-pleasing snack with a kick.

Servings: 4

Preparation Time: 15 minutes

Cooking Time: 12 minutes

Ingredients:

- 8 large jalapeños, halved and seeded
- 4 oz cream cheese, softened (115 g)
- 8 slices bacon, halved
- 1/2 teaspoon garlic powder (2.5 g)
- 1/4 teaspoon smoked paprika (1.5 g)

Directions:

1. Preheat the Ninja Foodi to 375°F (190°C).
2. Fill each jalapeño half with cream cheese.
3. Wrap each jalapeño half with a half slice of bacon and secure with a toothpick if necessary.
4. Place the bacon-wrapped jalapeños in one basket and air fry for 10-12 minutes until the bacon is crispy and the jalapeños are tender.
5. Serve hot.

10. Cheesy Garlic Breadsticks

Soft and cheesy breadsticks with a crispy garlic butter crust, perfect for dipping in marinara sauce.

Servings: 4

Preparation Time: 10 minutes

Cooking Time: 10 minutes

Ingredients:

- 1 can refrigerated pizza dough
- 2 tablespoons butter, melted (30 g)
- 2 cloves garlic, minced
- 1 cup shredded mozzarella cheese (120 g)
- 1/4 cup grated Parmesan cheese (30 g)
- 1 teaspoon dried oregano (5 g)
- Marinara sauce for dipping

Directions:

1. Preheat the Ninja Foodi to 375°F (190°C).
2. Roll out the pizza dough and cut into strips.
3. In a small bowl, mix melted butter with minced garlic.
4. Brush the dough strips with garlic butter and sprinkle with mozzarella, Parmesan, and dried oregano.
5. Place the breadsticks in one basket and air fry for 8-10 minutes until golden and the cheese is melted.
6. Serve with warm marinara sauce for dipping.

11. Zucchini Fritters

Light and crispy zucchini fritters that are perfect for a quick snack or appetizer, served with a dollop of sour cream or yogurt.

Servings: 4

Preparation Time: 10 minutes

Cooking Time: 12 minutes

Ingredients:

- 2 medium zucchinis, grated
- 1/2 cup all-purpose flour (60 g)
- 1/4 cup grated Parmesan cheese (30 g)
- 1 egg, beaten
- 2 green onions, finely chopped
- 1 teaspoon garlic powder (5 g)
- Salt and pepper to taste
- Olive oil spray

Directions:

1. Preheat the Ninja Foodi to 375°F (190°C).
2. Place the grated zucchini in a clean kitchen towel and squeeze out excess moisture.
3. In a bowl, mix the zucchini with flour, Parmesan, egg, green onions, garlic powder, salt, and pepper until well combined.
4. Form the mixture into small patties and spray with olive oil on both sides.
5. Place the fritters in one basket and air fry for 10-12 minutes until golden and crispy, flipping halfway through.
6. Serve hot with sour cream or yogurt.

12. Crispy Falafel Bites

These falafel bites are crispy on the outside and tender on the inside, perfect for dipping in tahini or hummus.

Servings: 4

Preparation Time: 15 minutes

Cooking Time: 10 minutes

Ingredients:

- 1 can chickpeas, drained and rinsed (15 oz, 425 g)
- 1/4 cup chopped parsley (15 g)

- 1/4 cup chopped cilantro (15 g)
- 1 small onion, chopped
- 2 cloves garlic, minced
- 1 teaspoon ground cumin (5 g)
- 1 teaspoon ground coriander (5 g)
- 1/2 teaspoon baking powder (2.5 g)
- 2 tablespoons all-purpose flour (30 g)
- Salt and pepper to taste
- Olive oil spray

Directions:
1. Preheat the Ninja Foodi to 375°F (190°C).
2. In a food processor, combine chickpeas, parsley, cilantro, onion, garlic, cumin, coriander, baking powder, flour, salt, and pepper. Pulse until the mixture is well combined but still slightly chunky.
3. Form the mixture into small balls or patties and spray with olive oil.
4. Place the falafel bites in one basket and air fry for 8-10 minutes until crispy, shaking the basket halfway through.
5. Serve with tahini or hummus for dipping.

13. Parmesan Truffle Fries

Crispy French fries tossed with Parmesan cheese and a hint of truffle oil for a gourmet twist on a classic snack.
Servings: 4
Preparation Time: 10 minutes
Cooking Time: 20 minutes
Ingredients:
- 2 large russet potatoes, cut into fries
- 2 tablespoons olive oil (30 ml)
- 1/4 cup grated Parmesan cheese (30 g)
- 1 tablespoon truffle oil (15 ml)
- 1 teaspoon garlic powder (5 g)
- Salt and pepper to taste

Directions:
1. Preheat the Ninja Foodi to 400°F (200°C).
2. Toss the potato fries with olive oil, garlic powder, salt, and pepper.
3. Place the fries in one basket and air fry for 18-20 minutes until golden and crispy, shaking the basket halfway through.
4. Transfer the fries to a bowl and toss with Parmesan cheese and truffle oil.

5. Serve hot as a delicious and indulgent snack.

14. Buffalo Chicken Bites

Spicy and flavorful buffalo chicken bites that are perfect for game day or any gathering.
Servings: 4
Preparation Time: 10 minutes
Cooking Time: 12 minutes
Ingredients:
- 1 lb boneless, skinless chicken breasts, cut into bite-sized pieces (450 g)
- 1/2 cup all-purpose flour (60 g)
- 1/2 teaspoon garlic powder (2.5 g)
- 1/2 teaspoon smoked paprika (2.5 g)
- 1/2 cup buffalo sauce (120 ml)
- 2 tablespoons butter, melted (30 g)
- Salt and pepper to taste

Directions:
1. Preheat the Ninja Foodi to 375°F (190°C).
2. In a bowl, mix the flour, garlic powder, smoked paprika, salt, and pepper.
3. Toss the chicken pieces in the flour mixture until evenly coated.
4. Place the chicken in one basket and air fry for 10-12 minutes until crispy, shaking the basket halfway through.
5. In a separate bowl, mix buffalo sauce with melted butter. Toss the hot chicken bites in the sauce.
6. Serve with celery sticks and blue cheese dressing.

15. Baked Stuffed Mushrooms

Savory mushrooms stuffed with a delicious mixture of cream cheese, garlic, and herbs, then baked to perfection.
Servings: 4
Preparation Time: 10 minutes
Cooking Time: 12 minutes
Ingredients:
- 16 large button mushrooms, stems removed
- 4 oz cream cheese, softened (115 g)
- 1/4 cup grated Parmesan cheese (30 g)
- 2 cloves garlic, minced

- 1 tablespoon chopped fresh parsley (optional, 5 g)
- Salt and pepper to taste

Directions:
1. Preheat the Ninja Foodi to 375°F (190°C).
2. In a bowl, mix the cream cheese, Parmesan cheese, garlic, parsley, salt, and pepper until well combined.
3. Spoon the mixture into the mushroom caps.
4. Place the stuffed mushrooms in one basket and air fry for 10-12 minutes until the mushrooms are tender and the tops are golden.
5. Serve hot as a savory appetizer.

16. Crispy Onion Rings

Golden and crispy onion rings with a perfectly seasoned coating, ideal for dipping in your favorite sauce.

Servings: 4
Preparation Time: 10 minutes
Cooking Time: 10 minutes
Ingredients:
- 2 large onions, sliced into rings
- 1 cup all-purpose flour (120 g)
- 2 eggs, beaten
- 1 cup panko breadcrumbs (120 g)
- 1 teaspoon smoked paprika (5 g)
- 1 teaspoon garlic powder (5 g)
- Salt and pepper to taste
- Olive oil spray

Directions:
1. Preheat the Ninja Foodi to 400°F (200°C).
2. Set up a breading station with three shallow dishes: one with flour, one with beaten eggs, and one with panko breadcrumbs mixed with smoked paprika, garlic powder, salt, and pepper.
3. Dredge each onion ring in flour, dip in the egg, and then coat with the breadcrumb mixture.
4. Place the onion rings in one basket and spray with olive oil. Air fry for 8-10 minutes until golden and crispy, shaking the basket halfway through.
5. Serve hot with your favorite dipping sauce.

17. Caprese Skewers

Fresh and simple Caprese skewers with mozzarella, cherry tomatoes, and basil, drizzled with balsamic glaze.

Servings: 4
Preparation Time: 10 minutes
Cooking Time: 0 minutes
Ingredients:
- 16 cherry tomatoes
- 16 mini mozzarella balls
- 16 fresh basil leaves
- 2 tablespoons balsamic glaze (30 ml)
- Salt and pepper to taste
- Wooden skewers

Directions:
1. Thread one cherry tomato, one mozzarella ball, and one basil leaf onto each skewer.
2. Arrange the skewers on a serving platter.
3. Drizzle with balsamic glaze and season with salt and pepper to taste.
4. Serve immediately as a fresh and elegant appetizer.

18. Crispy Avocado Fries

Creamy avocado slices coated in crunchy panko breadcrumbs, air-fried to perfection and served with a zesty dipping sauce.

Servings: 4
Preparation Time: 10 minutes
Cooking Time: 10 minutes
Ingredients:
- 2 ripe avocados, sliced
- 1/2 cup all-purpose flour (60 g)
- 2 eggs, beaten
- 1 cup panko breadcrumbs (120 g)
- 1/2 teaspoon garlic powder (2.5 g)
- Salt and pepper to taste
- Olive oil spray

Directions:
1. Preheat the Ninja Foodi to 375°F (190°C).
2. Set up a breading station with three shallow dishes: one with flour, one with beaten eggs, and one with panko breadcrumbs mixed with garlic powder, salt, and pepper.

3. Dredge each avocado slice in flour, dip in the egg, and then coat with the breadcrumb mixture.
4. Place the avocado slices in one basket and spray with olive oil. Air fry for 8-10 minutes until golden and crispy, shaking the basket halfway through.
5. Serve hot with your favorite dipping sauce.

19. Cheesy Cauliflower Bites

Bite-sized cauliflower florets coated in a cheesy breadcrumb mixture and baked until crispy and delicious.

Servings: 4
Preparation Time: 10 minutes
Cooking Time: 15 minutes
Ingredients:
- 1 head cauliflower, cut into small florets
- 1/2 cup grated Parmesan cheese (60 g)
- 1/2 cup panko breadcrumbs (60 g)
- 1/2 teaspoon garlic powder (2.5 g)
- 1/2 teaspoon smoked paprika (2.5 g)
- 1 egg, beaten
- Salt and pepper to taste
- Olive oil spray

Directions:
1. Preheat the Ninja Foodi to 375°F (190°C).
2. In a bowl, mix the Parmesan cheese, panko breadcrumbs, garlic powder, smoked paprika, salt, and pepper.
3. Dip each cauliflower floret in the beaten egg, then coat with the breadcrumb mixture.
4. Place the cauliflower bites in one basket and spray with olive oil. Air fry for 12-15 minutes until golden and crispy, shaking the basket halfway through.
5. Serve hot with marinara or ranch dressing.

20. Mini Caprese Pizzas

Bite-sized Caprese pizzas on mini naan bread, topped with fresh mozzarella, cherry tomatoes, and basil.

Servings: 4
Preparation Time: 10 minutes
Cooking Time: 8 minutes
Ingredients:
- 4 mini naan breads
- 1/2 cup marinara sauce (120 ml)
- 1 cup shredded mozzarella cheese (120 g)
- 8 cherry tomatoes, sliced
- 8 fresh basil leaves
- 1 tablespoon balsamic glaze (15 ml)
- Salt and pepper to taste

Directions:
1. Preheat the Ninja Foodi to 375°F (190°C).
2. Spread a layer of marinara sauce on each mini naan bread.
3. Top with shredded mozzarella, sliced cherry tomatoes, and fresh basil leaves.
4. Place the mini pizzas in one basket and air fry for 6-8 minutes until the cheese is melted and bubbly.
5. Drizzle with balsamic glaze and season with salt and pepper.
6. Serve immediately as a tasty and easy appetizer.

Chapter 11: Seafood Specialties

Seafood is a fantastic source of lean protein and essential nutrients, and with the Ninja Foodi 2-Basket Air Fryer, you can prepare it effortlessly. Whether you're craving something light and fresh or rich and flavorful, these seafood recipes will bring the taste of the ocean to your table. From crispy fish fillets to succulent shrimp dishes, each recipe is designed to be easy, healthy, and delicious.

1. Lemon Garlic Butter Shrimp

Juicy shrimp sautéed in a zesty lemon garlic butter sauce, perfect for a quick and flavorful dinner.

Servings: 4
Preparation Time: 10 minutes
Cooking Time: 10 minutes
Ingredients:

- 1 lb large shrimp, peeled and deveined (450 g)
- 3 tablespoons butter, melted (45 g)
- 3 cloves garlic, minced
- Juice of 1 lemon
- 1 tablespoon olive oil (15 ml)
- 1 teaspoon paprika (5 g)
- Salt and pepper to taste
- Fresh parsley, chopped (optional)

Directions:

1. Preheat the Ninja Foodi to 375°F (190°C).
2. In a bowl, toss the shrimp with melted butter, garlic, lemon juice, olive oil, paprika, salt, and pepper.
3. Place the shrimp in one basket in a single layer and air fry for 8-10 minutes until the shrimp are pink and cooked through, shaking the basket halfway through.
4. Garnish with chopped parsley if desired, and serve immediately.

2. Crispy Fish Tacos with Slaw

Crispy fish fillets served in warm tortillas with a crunchy slaw and tangy sauce, perfect for a fresh and tasty meal.

Servings: 4
Preparation Time: 15 minutes
Cooking Time: 12 minutes
Ingredients:

- 1 lb white fish fillets (e.g., cod, tilapia) (450 g)
- 1/2 cup all-purpose flour (60 g)
- 2 eggs, beaten
- 1 cup panko breadcrumbs (120 g)
- 1 teaspoon smoked paprika (5 g)
- 1/2 teaspoon garlic powder (2.5 g)
- Salt and pepper to taste
- 8 small corn tortillas
- 2 cups shredded cabbage (150 g)
- 1/4 cup mayonnaise (60 ml)
- 1 tablespoon lime juice (15 ml)
- 1 tablespoon chopped cilantro (optional, 5 g)

Directions:

1. Preheat the Ninja Foodi to 375°F (190°C).
2. Set up a breading station with three shallow dishes: one with flour, one with beaten eggs, and one with panko breadcrumbs mixed with smoked paprika, garlic powder, salt, and pepper.
3. Dredge each fish fillet in flour, dip in the egg, and then coat with the breadcrumb mixture.

4. Place the breaded fish fillets in one basket and air fry for 10-12 minutes until golden and crispy, flipping halfway through.
5. While the fish is cooking, mix the shredded cabbage, mayonnaise, lime juice, and cilantro in a bowl to make the slaw.
6. Warm the tortillas in the second basket for 2-3 minutes at 350°F (175°C).
7. Assemble the tacos by placing a piece of crispy fish on each tortilla and topping with slaw. Serve immediately.

3. Garlic Parmesan Crusted Salmon

Tender salmon fillets coated in a garlic Parmesan crust, making for a rich and flavorful dish that's ready in minutes.

Servings: 4
Preparation Time: 10 minutes
Cooking Time: 15 minutes
Ingredients:
- 4 salmon fillets (about 6 oz each, 170 g)
- 1/2 cup grated Parmesan cheese (60 g)
- 1/4 cup breadcrumbs (30 g)
- 2 cloves garlic, minced
- 2 tablespoons olive oil (30 ml)
- 1 teaspoon dried parsley (5 g)
- Salt and pepper to taste

Directions:
1. Preheat the Ninja Foodi to 375°F (190°C).
2. In a small bowl, mix Parmesan cheese, breadcrumbs, minced garlic, olive oil, parsley, salt, and pepper.
3. Press the Parmesan mixture onto the top of each salmon fillet.
4. Place the salmon fillets in one basket and air fry for 12-15 minutes until the topping is golden and the salmon is cooked through.
5. Serve hot with a side of vegetables or salad.

4. Coconut Crusted Mahi-Mahi

Mahi-Mahi fillets coated in a sweet and crispy coconut crust, bringing a taste of the tropics to your dinner table.

Servings: 4
Preparation Time: 15 minutes
Cooking Time: 12 minutes
Ingredients:
- 4 Mahi-Mahi fillets (about 6 oz each, 170 g)
- 1/2 cup shredded coconut (50 g)
- 1/4 cup panko breadcrumbs (30 g)
- 1/4 cup all-purpose flour (30 g)
- 2 eggs, beaten
- 1/2 teaspoon salt (2.5 g)
- 1/4 teaspoon black pepper (1.5 g)
- 1/4 teaspoon cayenne pepper (1.5 g) (optional)

Directions:
1. Preheat the Ninja Foodi to 375°F (190°C).
2. In three separate shallow dishes, place the flour, beaten eggs, and a mixture of shredded coconut, panko breadcrumbs, salt, black pepper, and cayenne pepper.
3. Dredge each Mahi-Mahi fillet in flour, dip in the egg, and then coat with the coconut mixture.
4. Place the fillets in one basket and air fry for 10-12 minutes until the coconut is golden and the fish is cooked through, flipping halfway through.
5. Serve with a side of rice and a squeeze of fresh lime.

5. Cajun Shrimp and Sausage Skewers

Spicy Cajun-seasoned shrimp and sausage skewers that are perfect for grilling or air frying, delivering bold flavors in every bite.

Servings: 4
Preparation Time: 15 minutes
Cooking Time: 10 minutes
Ingredients:
- 1 lb large shrimp, peeled and deveined (450 g)
- 8 oz smoked sausage, sliced into 1/2-inch pieces (225 g)
- 2 tablespoons olive oil (30 ml)
- 1 tablespoon Cajun seasoning (15 g)

- 1 teaspoon garlic powder (5 g)
- Wooden or metal skewers

Directions:
1. Preheat the Ninja Foodi to 375°F (190°C).
2. In a large bowl, toss the shrimp and sausage pieces with olive oil, Cajun seasoning, and garlic powder.
3. Thread the shrimp and sausage alternately onto skewers.
4. Place the skewers in one basket and air fry for 8-10 minutes until the shrimp are pink and cooked through, flipping halfway through.
5. Serve with a side of coleslaw or over rice.

6. Lemon Herb Grilled Scallops

Perfectly seared scallops with a bright lemon herb marinade, offering a simple yet elegant seafood dish.

Servings: 4
Preparation Time: 10 minutes
Cooking Time: 8 minutes
Ingredients:
- 1 lb large sea scallops (450 g)
- 2 tablespoons olive oil (30 ml)
- Juice of 1 lemon
- 2 cloves garlic, minced
- 1 teaspoon dried thyme (5 g)
- 1 teaspoon dried oregano (5 g)
- Salt and pepper to taste

Directions:
1. Preheat the Ninja Foodi to 400°F (200°C).
2. In a bowl, toss the scallops with olive oil, lemon juice, garlic, thyme, oregano, salt, and pepper.
3. Place the scallops in one basket in a single layer and air fry for 6-8 minutes until they are golden brown and opaque, flipping halfway through.
4. Serve with a lemon wedge and a side of steamed vegetables or pasta.

7. Blackened Catfish

Spicy and flavorful blackened catfish, seared to perfection and served with a side of rice or greens.

Servings: 4
Preparation Time: 10 minutes
Cooking Time: 10 minutes

Ingredients:
- 4 catfish fillets (about 6 oz each, 170 g)
- 2 tablespoons olive oil (30 ml)
- 1 tablespoon Cajun seasoning (15 g)
- 1 teaspoon smoked paprika (5 g)
- 1/2 teaspoon garlic powder (2.5 g)
- Salt and pepper to taste

Directions:
1. Preheat the Ninja Foodi to 400°F (200°C).
2. Brush the catfish fillets with olive oil and season with Cajun seasoning, smoked paprika, garlic powder, salt, and pepper.
3. Place the fillets in one basket and air fry for 8-10 minutes until the fish is flaky and the spices are blackened, flipping halfway through.
4. Serve with a side of rice or sautéed greens.

8. Garlic Butter Lobster Tails

Luxurious lobster tails basted in garlic butter and air-fried to tender perfection, making for an indulgent meal.

Servings: 4
Preparation Time: 10 minutes
Cooking Time: 10 minutes
Ingredients:
- 4 lobster tails (about 6 oz each, 170 g)
- 4 tablespoons butter, melted (60 g)
- 2 cloves garlic, minced
- Juice of 1 lemon
- 1 tablespoon chopped fresh parsley (optional, 5 g)
- Salt and pepper to taste

Directions:
1. Preheat the Ninja Foodi to 375°F (190°C).
2. Using kitchen shears, carefully cut the top of each lobster shell lengthwise and pull the meat up, resting it on top of the shell.
3. In a small bowl, mix melted butter, minced garlic, lemon juice, salt, and pepper.
4. Brush the lobster meat with the garlic butter mixture.
5. Place the lobster tails in one basket and air fry for 8-10 minutes until the meat is opaque and cooked through.

6. Garnish with chopped parsley and serve with additional garlic butter for dipping.

9. Sesame Crusted Tuna Steaks

Ahi tuna steaks coated in sesame seeds and seared to perfection, served rare with a side of soy dipping sauce.

Servings: 4
Preparation Time: 10 minutes
Cooking Time: 8 minutes
Ingredients:

- 4 ahi tuna steaks (about 6 oz each, 170 g)
- 1/4 cup sesame seeds (30 g)
- 2 tablespoons soy sauce (30 ml)
- 1 tablespoon olive oil (15 ml)
- 1 tablespoon rice vinegar (15 ml)
- 1 teaspoon sesame oil (5 ml)
- Salt and pepper to taste

Directions:

1. Preheat the Ninja Foodi to 400°F (200°C).
2. In a small bowl, mix soy sauce, olive oil, rice vinegar, sesame oil, salt, and pepper.
3. Coat the tuna steaks with the marinade, then press sesame seeds onto both sides of each steak.
4. Place the tuna steaks in one basket and air fry for 6-8 minutes until the sesame seeds are toasted and the tuna is seared on the outside but still rare inside.
5. Serve with a side of soy dipping sauce and steamed rice or salad.

10. Shrimp Scampi

Classic shrimp scampi with a buttery garlic sauce and a hint of lemon, served over pasta or with crusty bread.

Servings: 4
Preparation Time: 10 minutes
Cooking Time: 10 minutes
Ingredients:

- 1 lb large shrimp, peeled and deveined (450 g)
- 4 tablespoons butter, melted (60 g)
- 3 cloves garlic, minced
- Juice of 1 lemon
- 1/4 cup white wine (60 ml) (optional)
- 1 tablespoon chopped fresh parsley (5 g)
- Salt and pepper to taste

- Cooked pasta or crusty bread for serving

Directions:

1. Preheat the Ninja Foodi to 375°F (190°C).
2. In a bowl, toss the shrimp with melted butter, garlic, lemon juice, white wine (if using), salt, and pepper.
3. Place the shrimp in one basket in a single layer and air fry for 8-10 minutes until the shrimp are pink and cooked through, shaking the basket halfway through.
4. Garnish with chopped parsley and serve over pasta or with crusty bread for dipping in the garlic butter sauce.

11. Spicy Sriracha Grilled Shrimp

Succulent shrimp marinated in a spicy Sriracha sauce and grilled to perfection, delivering a burst of flavor with every bite.

Servings: 4
Preparation Time: 15 minutes
Cooking Time: 10 minutes
Ingredients:

- 1 lb large shrimp, peeled and deveined (450 g)
- 2 tablespoons Sriracha sauce (30 ml)
- 2 tablespoons soy sauce (30 ml)
- 1 tablespoon honey (15 ml)
- 1 tablespoon olive oil (15 ml)
- 1 clove garlic, minced
- Juice of 1 lime
- Wooden or metal skewers

Directions:

1. In a large bowl, whisk together Sriracha, soy sauce, honey, olive oil, garlic, and lime juice.
2. Add the shrimp to the marinade and toss to coat. Let it marinate for 15-30 minutes.
3. Preheat the Ninja Foodi to 375°F (190°C).
4. Thread the shrimp onto skewers and place them in one basket.
5. Air fry for 8-10 minutes until the shrimp are cooked through, flipping halfway through.
6. Serve hot with extra lime wedges.

12. Lemon Dill Baked Cod

Tender cod fillets seasoned with lemon and fresh dill, baked until flaky and light, making for a simple yet elegant dish.

Servings: 4
Preparation Time: 10 minutes
Cooking Time: 12 minutes
Ingredients:

- 4 cod fillets (about 6 oz each, 170 g)
- 2 tablespoons olive oil (30 ml)
- Juice of 1 lemon
- 2 tablespoons fresh dill, chopped (10 g)
- Salt and pepper to taste
- Lemon wedges for serving

Directions:

1. Preheat the Ninja Foodi to 375°F (190°C).
2. In a small bowl, mix olive oil, lemon juice, dill, salt, and pepper.
3. Brush the cod fillets with the lemon dill mixture.
4. Place the fillets in one basket and air fry for 10-12 minutes until the fish is flaky and cooked through.
5. Serve with additional lemon wedges and a side of steamed vegetables.

13. Crispy Coconut Shrimp with Mango Salsa

Golden, crispy shrimp coated in coconut and served with a refreshing mango salsa for a tropical twist on a seafood classic.

Servings: 4
Preparation Time: 20 minutes
Cooking Time: 10 minutes
Ingredients:

- 1 lb large shrimp, peeled and deveined (450 g)
- 1/2 cup all-purpose flour (60 g)
- 2 eggs, beaten
- 1 cup shredded coconut (100 g)
- 1/2 cup panko breadcrumbs (60 g)
- 1/2 teaspoon salt (2.5 g)
- 1/4 teaspoon black pepper (1.5 g)
- 1 ripe mango, diced
- 1/4 red onion, finely chopped
- 1/4 cup fresh cilantro, chopped (15 g)
- Juice of 1 lime

Directions:

1. Preheat the Ninja Foodi to 375°F (190°C).
2. In three shallow dishes, place flour, beaten eggs, and a mixture of shredded coconut, panko breadcrumbs, salt, and pepper.
3. Dredge each shrimp in flour, dip in egg, and coat with the coconut mixture.
4. Place the shrimp in one basket and air fry for 8-10 minutes until golden and crispy.
5. While the shrimp cooks, mix mango, red onion, cilantro, and lime juice in a bowl to make the salsa.
6. Serve the shrimp with the mango salsa on the side.

14. Herb Crusted Tilapia

Light and flaky tilapia fillets with a crispy herb crust, perfect for a quick and healthy meal.

Servings: 4
Preparation Time: 10 minutes
Cooking Time: 10 minutes
Ingredients:

- 4 tilapia fillets (about 6 oz each, 170 g)
- 1/2 cup panko breadcrumbs (60 g)
- 1/4 cup grated Parmesan cheese (30 g)
- 1 tablespoon fresh parsley, chopped (5 g)
- 1 tablespoon olive oil (15 ml)
- 1 teaspoon dried thyme (5 g)
- 1/2 teaspoon garlic powder (2.5 g)
- Salt and pepper to taste

Directions:

1. Preheat the Ninja Foodi to 375°F (190°C).
2. In a bowl, mix panko breadcrumbs, Parmesan cheese, parsley, olive oil, thyme, garlic powder, salt, and pepper.
3. Press the breadcrumb mixture onto the top of each tilapia fillet.
4. Place the fillets in one basket and air fry for 8-10 minutes until the crust is golden and the fish is cooked through.
5. Serve with a squeeze of fresh lemon juice and a side of vegetables.

15. Grilled Swordfish Steaks with Chimichurri

Meaty swordfish steaks grilled to perfection and topped with a vibrant and tangy chimichurri sauce.

Servings: 4
Preparation Time: 15 minutes
Cooking Time: 12 minutes
Ingredients:

- 4 swordfish steaks (about 6 oz each, 170 g)
- 2 tablespoons olive oil (30 ml)
- Salt and pepper to taste
- 1/2 cup fresh parsley, chopped (30 g)
- 1/4 cup fresh cilantro, chopped (15 g)
- 2 cloves garlic, minced
- 1/4 cup red wine vinegar (60 ml)
- 1/4 cup olive oil (60 ml)
- 1/2 teaspoon red pepper flakes (2.5 g)
- Juice of 1 lemon

Directions:

1. Preheat the Ninja Foodi to 375°F (190°C).
2. Brush the swordfish steaks with olive oil and season with salt and pepper.
3. Place the steaks in one basket and air fry for 10-12 minutes until the fish is cooked through, flipping halfway through.
4. While the fish cooks, mix parsley, cilantro, garlic, red wine vinegar, olive oil, red pepper flakes, and lemon juice in a bowl to make the chimichurri.
5. Serve the swordfish steaks topped with chimichurri sauce.

16. Dijon Baked Salmon

Salmon fillets coated with a tangy Dijon mustard glaze and baked to perfection, resulting in a rich and flavorful dish.

Servings: 4
Preparation Time: 10 minutes
Cooking Time: 12 minutes
Ingredients:

- 4 salmon fillets (about 6 oz each, 170 g)
- 2 tablespoons Dijon mustard (30 g)
- 1 tablespoon honey (15 ml)
- 1 tablespoon olive oil (15 ml)
- 1 teaspoon dried thyme (5 g)
- Salt and pepper to taste
- Lemon wedges for serving

Directions:

1. Preheat the Ninja Foodi to 375°F (190°C).
2. In a small bowl, mix Dijon mustard, honey, olive oil, thyme, salt, and pepper.
3. Brush the mustard mixture over the salmon fillets.
4. Place the fillets in one basket and air fry for 10-12 minutes until the salmon is cooked through.
5. Serve with lemon wedges and a side of green beans or roasted potatoes.

17. Crispy Calamari Rings

Tender calamari rings coated in a light, crispy batter and served with a zesty marinara sauce for dipping.

Servings: 4
Preparation Time: 15 minutes
Cooking Time: 8 minutes
Ingredients:

- 1 lb calamari rings (450 g)
- 1/2 cup all-purpose flour (60 g)
- 1/4 cup cornstarch (30 g)
- 1 teaspoon garlic powder (5 g)
- 1/2 teaspoon smoked paprika (2.5 g)
- Salt and pepper to taste
- 1 egg, beaten
- Olive oil spray
- Marinara sauce for serving

Directions:

1. Preheat the Ninja Foodi to 400°F (200°C).
2. In a shallow dish, mix flour, cornstarch, garlic powder, smoked paprika, salt, and pepper.
3. Dip each calamari ring in the beaten egg, then coat with the flour mixture.
4. Place the calamari in one basket, spray with olive oil, and air fry for 6-8 minutes until golden and crispy, shaking the basket halfway through.
5. Serve hot with marinara sauce.

18. Teriyaki Glazed Salmon

Sweet and savory teriyaki glazed salmon fillets, cooked to perfection and served with steamed rice or vegetables.

Servings: 4

Preparation Time: 10 minutes

Cooking Time: 12 minutes

Ingredients:

- 4 salmon fillets (about 6 oz each, 170 g)
- 1/4 cup soy sauce (60 ml)
- 2 tablespoons honey (30 ml)
- 1 tablespoon rice vinegar (15 ml)
- 1 teaspoon sesame oil (5 ml)
- 1 clove garlic, minced
- 1 teaspoon grated fresh ginger (5 g)
- 1 tablespoon sesame seeds (optional, 15 g)
- Sliced green onions for garnish

Directions:

1. Preheat the Ninja Foodi to 375°F (190°C).
2. In a small bowl, mix soy sauce, honey, rice vinegar, sesame oil, garlic, and ginger.
3. Brush the salmon fillets with the teriyaki glaze.
4. Place the fillets in one basket and air fry for 10-12 minutes until the salmon is cooked through.
5. Sprinkle with sesame seeds and garnish with sliced green onions. Serve with steamed rice.

19. Garlic Butter Mussels

Steamed mussels in a rich garlic butter sauce, perfect for serving with crusty bread to soak up the flavorful broth.

Servings: 4

Preparation Time: 10 minutes

Cooking Time: 10 minutes

Ingredients:

- 2 lbs fresh mussels, cleaned and debearded (900 g)
- 4 tablespoons butter, melted (60 g)
- 4 cloves garlic, minced
- 1/4 cup white wine (60 ml)
- 1/4 cup fresh parsley, chopped (15 g)
- Juice of 1 lemon
- Salt and pepper to taste

Directions:

1. Preheat the Ninja Foodi to 375°F (190°C).
2. In a large bowl, toss the mussels with melted butter, garlic, white wine, lemon juice, salt, and pepper.
3. Place the mussels in one basket and air fry for 8-10 minutes until the mussels open up and are cooked through, shaking the basket halfway through.
4. Garnish with chopped parsley and serve with crusty bread.

20. Grilled Shrimp Caesar Salad

Juicy grilled shrimp served on a bed of crisp romaine lettuce, tossed with Caesar dressing, croutons, and Parmesan cheese.

Servings: 4

Preparation Time: 15 minutes

Cooking Time: 10 minutes

Ingredients:

- 1 lb large shrimp, peeled and deveined (450 g)
- 2 tablespoons olive oil (30 ml)
- 1 teaspoon garlic powder (5 g)
- 1 teaspoon smoked paprika (5 g)
- Salt and pepper to taste
- 4 cups romaine lettuce, chopped (200 g)
- 1/4 cup Caesar dressing (60 ml)
- 1/4 cup grated Parmesan cheese (30 g)
- 1/2 cup croutons (30 g)
- Lemon wedges for serving

Directions:

1. Preheat the Ninja Foodi to 375°F (190°C).
2. Toss the shrimp with olive oil, garlic powder, smoked paprika, salt, and pepper.
3. Place the shrimp in one basket and air fry for 8-10 minutes until the shrimp are pink and cooked through.
4. In a large bowl, toss the romaine lettuce with Caesar dressing, Parmesan cheese, and croutons.
5. Top the salad with grilled shrimp and serve with lemon wedges.

Chapter 12: Poultry Perfection

Chicken and turkey are staples in many households, and with the Ninja Foodi 2-Basket Air Fryer, you can prepare these proteins in a variety of delicious ways. Whether you're in the mood for something classic or want to try a new flavor, these poultry recipes will help you make the most of your kitchen gadget. Each recipe is designed to be easy to follow, healthy, and, most importantly, full of flavor.

1. Herb-Crusted Chicken Thighs

Juicy chicken thighs coated in a flavorful herb crust, air-fried to crispy perfection for a comforting meal.

Servings: 4
Preparation Time: 10 minutes
Cooking Time: 25 minutes
Ingredients:

- 1.5 lbs chicken thighs, bone-in, skin-on (680 g)
- 1/2 cup panko breadcrumbs (60 g)
- 1/4 cup grated Parmesan cheese (30 g)
- 1 teaspoon dried rosemary (5 g)
- 1 teaspoon dried thyme (5 g)
- 1/2 teaspoon garlic powder (2.5 g)
- Salt and pepper to taste
- 2 tablespoons olive oil (30 ml)

Directions:

1. Preheat the Ninja Foodi to 375°F (190°C).
2. In a shallow dish, combine panko breadcrumbs, Parmesan cheese, rosemary, thyme, garlic powder, salt, and pepper.
3. Rub the chicken thighs with olive oil and press them into the breadcrumb mixture to coat.
4. Place the chicken thighs in one basket, skin-side up, and air fry for 25 minutes until the chicken is golden and cooked through, flipping halfway through.
5. Serve hot with your favorite side dishes.

2. Honey Mustard Chicken Breasts

Tender chicken breasts glazed with a sweet and tangy honey mustard sauce, perfect for a quick weeknight dinner.

Servings: 4
Preparation Time: 10 minutes
Cooking Time: 20 minutes
Ingredients:

- 1.5 lbs chicken breasts (680 g)
- 1/4 cup honey (60 ml)
- 1/4 cup Dijon mustard (60 ml)
- 2 tablespoons olive oil (30 ml)
- 2 cloves garlic, minced
- 1 teaspoon dried thyme (5 g)
- Salt and pepper to taste

Directions:

1. Preheat the Ninja Foodi to 375°F (190°C).
2. In a small bowl, whisk together honey, Dijon mustard, olive oil, garlic, thyme, salt, and pepper.
3. Brush the chicken breasts with the honey mustard mixture, reserving some for basting.
4. Place the chicken breasts in one basket and air fry for 18-20 minutes until cooked through, basting with the remaining sauce halfway through.
5. Serve with a side of roasted vegetables or a fresh salad.

3. Buffalo Chicken Wings

Classic buffalo chicken wings with a spicy kick, perfect for game day or any casual gathering.

Servings: 4
Preparation Time: 10 minutes
Cooking Time: 25 minutes
Ingredients:

- 2 lbs chicken wings, split and tips removed (900 g)
- 2 tablespoons olive oil (30 ml)
- 1/2 cup buffalo sauce (120 ml)
- 2 tablespoons butter, melted (30 g)
- 1 teaspoon garlic powder (5 g)
- Salt and pepper to taste

Directions:

1. Preheat the Ninja Foodi to 400°F (200°C).
2. Toss the chicken wings with olive oil, garlic powder, salt, and pepper.
3. Place the wings in one basket and air fry for 20-25 minutes until crispy, shaking the basket halfway through.
4. In a separate bowl, mix buffalo sauce with melted butter. Toss the hot wings in the sauce.
5. Serve with celery sticks and blue cheese dressing.

4. Lemon Herb Roast Chicken

A whole roasted chicken seasoned with fresh herbs and lemon, creating a tender and flavorful dish.

Servings: 4-6
Preparation Time: 15 minutes
Cooking Time: 60 minutes
Ingredients:

- 1 whole chicken (about 4 lbs, 1.8 kg)
- 1/4 cup olive oil (60 ml)
- Juice of 2 lemons
- 4 cloves garlic, minced
- 2 tablespoons fresh rosemary, chopped (10 g)
- 2 tablespoons fresh thyme, chopped (10 g)
- Salt and pepper to taste
- Lemon wedges for serving

Directions:

1. Preheat the Ninja Foodi to 375°F (190°C).
2. In a small bowl, mix olive oil, lemon juice, garlic, rosemary, thyme, salt, and pepper.
3. Rub the mixture all over the chicken, including under the skin.
4. Place the chicken in one basket, breast side down, and air fry for 30 minutes. Flip the chicken and continue to air fry for another 30 minutes until the internal temperature reaches 165°F (74°C).
5. Let the chicken rest for 10 minutes before carving. Serve with lemon wedges.

5. Teriyaki Chicken Skewers

Juicy chicken skewers marinated in a savory teriyaki sauce, grilled to perfection for a delicious meal.

Servings: 4
Preparation Time: 15 minutes (plus 2 hours for marinating)
Cooking Time: 15 minutes
Ingredients:

- 1.5 lbs chicken breast, cut into 1-inch cubes (680 g)
- 1/4 cup soy sauce (60 ml)
- 2 tablespoons honey (30 ml)
- 2 tablespoons rice vinegar (30 ml)
- 1 tablespoon sesame oil (15 ml)
- 2 cloves garlic, minced
- 1 teaspoon grated fresh ginger (5 g)
- Wooden or metal skewers

Directions:

1. In a large bowl, combine soy sauce, honey, rice vinegar, sesame oil, garlic, and ginger. Add the chicken cubes and mix well to coat. Cover and refrigerate for at least 2 hours, preferably overnight.
2. If using wooden skewers, soak them in water for 30 minutes to prevent burning. Thread the marinated chicken cubes onto the skewers, leaving a little space between each piece.
3. Preheat the Ninja Foodi to 375°F (190°C). Grill the skewers for 12-15 minutes, turning occasionally, until the chicken is fully cooked and has nice grill marks.
4. Serve with steamed rice and vegetables.

6. Crispy Chicken Parmesan

Breaded chicken breasts topped with marinara sauce and melted mozzarella, making for a comforting Italian classic.

Servings: 4
Preparation Time: 15 minutes
Cooking Time: 20 minutes
Ingredients:

- 1.5 lbs chicken breasts, pounded thin (680 g)
- 1/2 cup all-purpose flour (60 g)
- 2 eggs, beaten
- 1 cup panko breadcrumbs (120 g)
- 1/2 cup grated Parmesan cheese (60 g)
- 1 teaspoon dried oregano (5 g)
- 1 teaspoon garlic powder (5 g)
- 1/2 teaspoon salt (2.5 g)
- 1/4 teaspoon black pepper (1.5 g)
- 1 cup marinara sauce (240 ml)
- 1 cup shredded mozzarella cheese (120 g)
- Fresh basil leaves for garnish (optional)

Directions:

1. Preheat the Ninja Foodi to 375°F (190°C).
2. Set up a breading station with three shallow dishes: one with flour, one with beaten eggs, and one with panko breadcrumbs mixed with Parmesan cheese, oregano, garlic powder, salt, and pepper.
3. Dredge each chicken breast in flour, dip in the egg, and then coat with the breadcrumb mixture.
4. Place the breaded chicken breasts in one basket and air fry for 15 minutes until golden and crispy.
5. Top each chicken breast with marinara sauce and shredded mozzarella cheese. Air fry for an additional 3-5 minutes until the cheese is melted and bubbly.
6. Garnish with fresh basil leaves and serve with pasta or a side salad.

7. Greek Chicken Gyros

Flavorful chicken marinated in Greek herbs and spices, served in warm pita bread with fresh vegetables and tzatziki sauce.

Servings: 4
Preparation Time: 20 minutes (plus 2 hours for marinating)
Cooking Time: 15 minutes
Ingredients:

- 1.5 lbs chicken thighs, boneless and skinless (680 g)
- 1/4 cup olive oil (60 ml)
- 2 tablespoons lemon juice (30 ml)
- 2 cloves garlic, minced
- 1 teaspoon dried oregano (5 g)
- 1 teaspoon dried thyme (5 g)
- 1/2 teaspoon cumin (2.5 g)
- Salt and pepper to taste
- 4 pita breads
- Sliced tomatoes, cucumbers, red onions
- Tzatziki sauce for serving

Directions:

1. In a large bowl, mix olive oil, lemon juice, garlic, oregano, thyme, cumin, salt, and pepper. Add the chicken thighs and toss to coat. Cover and refrigerate for at least 2 hours, preferably overnight.
2. Preheat the Ninja Foodi to 375°F (190°C).
3. Place the chicken thighs in one basket and air fry for 12-15 minutes until fully cooked and golden brown, flipping halfway through.
4. Slice the chicken and serve in warm pita bread with sliced tomatoes, cucumbers, red onions, and a generous dollop of tzatziki sauce.

8. BBQ Chicken Drumsticks

Juicy chicken drumsticks smothered in tangy BBQ sauce and air-fried until tender and caramelized.

Servings: 4
Preparation Time: 10 minutes
Cooking Time: 25 minutes
Ingredients:

- 2 lbs chicken drumsticks (900 g)
- 1/2 cup BBQ sauce (120 ml)
- 2 tablespoons olive oil (30 ml)

- 1 teaspoon smoked paprika (5 g)
- 1 teaspoon garlic powder (5 g)
- Salt and pepper to taste

Directions:
1. Preheat the Ninja Foodi to 375°F (190°C).
2. Toss the chicken drumsticks with olive oil, smoked paprika, garlic powder, salt, and pepper.
3. Place the drumsticks in one basket and air fry for 20 minutes.
4. Brush the drumsticks with BBQ sauce and air fry for an additional 5 minutes until the sauce is caramelized.
5. Serve hot with coleslaw or potato salad.

9. Thai Peanut Chicken

Chicken breasts cooked in a rich and creamy Thai peanut sauce, served with jasmine rice and steamed vegetables.

Servings: 4
Preparation Time: 15 minutes
Cooking Time: 20 minutes
Ingredients:
- 1.5 lbs chicken breasts, sliced thinly (680 g)
- 1/4 cup peanut butter (60 g)
- 2 tablespoons soy sauce (30 ml)
- 2 tablespoons lime juice (30 ml)
- 1 tablespoon honey (15 ml)
- 1 tablespoon sesame oil (15 ml)
- 1 tablespoon sriracha sauce (15 ml) (optional)
- 2 cloves garlic, minced
- 1 teaspoon grated fresh ginger (5 g)
- Chopped peanuts and cilantro for garnish

Directions:
1. In a small bowl, mix peanut butter, soy sauce, lime juice, honey, sesame oil, sriracha sauce (if using), garlic, and ginger to make the sauce.
2. Preheat the Ninja Foodi to 375°F (190°C).
3. Toss the chicken slices with half of the peanut sauce.
4. Place the chicken in one basket and air fry for 15-20 minutes until cooked through, shaking the basket halfway through.

5. Serve the chicken over jasmine rice, drizzle with the remaining peanut sauce, and garnish with chopped peanuts and cilantro.

10. Orange Glazed Turkey Tenderloins

Tender turkey tenderloins glazed with a sweet and tangy orange sauce, perfect for a festive meal.

Servings: 4
Preparation Time: 15 minutes
Cooking Time: 20 minutes
Ingredients:
- 1.5 lbs turkey tenderloins (680 g)
- 1/2 cup orange juice (120 ml)
- 2 tablespoons honey (30 ml)
- 1 tablespoon soy sauce (15 ml)
- 1 tablespoon olive oil (15 ml)
- 1 clove garlic, minced
- 1 teaspoon grated orange zest (5 g)
- 1/2 teaspoon ground ginger (2.5 g)
- Salt and pepper to taste

Directions:
1. In a small bowl, mix orange juice, honey, soy sauce, olive oil, garlic, orange zest, ground ginger, salt, and pepper.
2. Preheat the Ninja Foodi to 375°F (190°C).
3. Brush the turkey tenderloins with the orange glaze.
4. Place the tenderloins in one basket and air fry for 15-20 minutes, basting with more glaze halfway through, until the turkey is cooked through and the glaze is caramelized.
5. Let the turkey rest for 5 minutes before slicing. Serve with roasted vegetables or a fresh salad.

11. Garlic Butter Chicken Thighs

Juicy chicken thighs cooked in a rich garlic butter sauce, creating a flavorful and comforting dish.

Servings: 4
Preparation Time: 10 minutes
Cooking Time: 25 minutes

Ingredients:
- 1.5 lbs chicken thighs, bone-in, skin-on (680 g)
- 4 tablespoons butter, melted (60 g)
- 4 cloves garlic, minced

- 1 teaspoon dried thyme (5 g)
- 1 teaspoon dried rosemary (5 g)
- Salt and pepper to taste
- Fresh parsley, chopped (optional)

Directions:
1. Preheat the Ninja Foodi to 375°F (190°C).
2. In a small bowl, mix melted butter, garlic, thyme, rosemary, salt, and pepper.
3. Brush the chicken thighs with the garlic butter mixture, making sure to coat under the skin as well.
4. Place the chicken thighs in one basket, skin-side up, and air fry for 25 minutes until golden brown and cooked through, flipping halfway through.
5. Garnish with chopped parsley and serve with mashed potatoes or steamed vegetables.

12. Moroccan-Spiced Chicken Breasts

Chicken breasts marinated in a blend of Moroccan spices, air-fried to tender perfection, and served with couscous.

Servings: 4
Preparation Time: 15 minutes (plus 2 hours for marinating)
Cooking Time: 20 minutes
Ingredients:
- 1.5 lbs chicken breasts (680 g)
- 2 tablespoons olive oil (30 ml)
- 1 tablespoon lemon juice (15 ml)
- 1 teaspoon ground cumin (5 g)
- 1 teaspoon ground coriander (5 g)
- 1 teaspoon paprika (5 g)
- 1/2 teaspoon ground cinnamon (2.5 g)
- 1/2 teaspoon ground turmeric (2.5 g)
- 2 cloves garlic, minced
- Salt and pepper to taste

Directions:
1. In a large bowl, mix olive oil, lemon juice, cumin, coriander, paprika, cinnamon, turmeric, garlic, salt, and pepper. Add the chicken breasts and toss to coat. Cover and refrigerate for at least 2 hours, preferably overnight.
2. Preheat the Ninja Foodi to 375°F (190°C).

3. Place the chicken breasts in one basket and air fry for 18-20 minutes until cooked through, flipping halfway through.
4. Serve with couscous and a side of roasted vegetables.

13. Pesto-Stuffed Chicken Breasts

Chicken breasts stuffed with a flavorful basil pesto and mozzarella cheese, creating a delicious and cheesy main course.

Servings: 4
Preparation Time: 15 minutes
Cooking Time: 20 minutes
Ingredients:
- 4 chicken breasts (about 6 oz each, 170 g)
- 1/2 cup basil pesto (120 g)
- 1 cup shredded mozzarella cheese (120 g)
- 2 tablespoons olive oil (30 ml)
- Salt and pepper to taste
- Toothpicks for securing

Directions:
1. Preheat the Ninja Foodi to 375°F (190°C).
2. Using a sharp knife, cut a pocket into the side of each chicken breast.
3. Stuff each pocket with a spoonful of pesto and shredded mozzarella cheese. Secure with toothpicks.
4. Brush the chicken breasts with olive oil and season with salt and pepper.
5. Place the stuffed chicken breasts in one basket and air fry for 18-20 minutes until the chicken is cooked through and the cheese is melted.
6. Serve with a side of roasted tomatoes or a fresh salad.

14. BBQ Chicken Quesadillas

Crispy quesadillas filled with BBQ chicken, melted cheese, and caramelized onions, perfect for a quick and satisfying meal.

Servings: 4
Preparation Time: 10 minutes
Cooking Time: 10 minutes
Ingredients:
- 2 cups cooked chicken, shredded (300 g)
- 1/2 cup BBQ sauce (120 ml)

- 1 cup shredded cheddar cheese (120 g)
- 1/2 cup caramelized onions (optional, 60 g)
- 4 large flour tortillas
- Olive oil spray

Directions:
1. Preheat the Ninja Foodi to 375°F (190°C).
2. In a bowl, mix the shredded chicken with BBQ sauce.
3. Place a tortilla on a flat surface and sprinkle half of it with shredded cheese, BBQ chicken, and caramelized onions.
4. Fold the tortilla in half to cover the filling.
5. Spray the quesadilla lightly with olive oil and place in one basket. Air fry for 5 minutes on each side until golden and crispy.
6. Slice into wedges and serve with sour cream or guacamole.

15. Lemon Pepper Turkey Meatballs

Juicy turkey meatballs seasoned with lemon pepper, served with a light and tangy yogurt sauce.

Servings: 4
Preparation Time: 15 minutes
Cooking Time: 15 minutes
Ingredients:
- 1 lb ground turkey (450 g)
- 1/2 cup breadcrumbs (60 g)
- 1 egg, beaten
- 2 cloves garlic, minced
- 1 tablespoon lemon zest (15 g)
- 1 teaspoon black pepper (5 g)
- 1/2 teaspoon salt (2.5 g)
- 2 tablespoons olive oil (30 ml)
- 1/2 cup plain Greek yogurt (120 ml)
- 1 tablespoon lemon juice (15 ml)
- 1 tablespoon fresh dill, chopped (optional, 5 g)

Directions:
1. Preheat the Ninja Foodi to 375°F (190°C).
2. In a large bowl, mix ground turkey, breadcrumbs, egg, garlic, lemon zest, black pepper, and salt until well combined. Form the mixture into small meatballs.
3. Brush the meatballs with olive oil and place them in one basket. Air fry for 12-15 minutes

until cooked through, shaking the basket halfway through.
4. In a small bowl, mix Greek yogurt, lemon juice, and dill (if using) to make the dipping sauce.
5. Serve the meatballs with the yogurt sauce on the side.

16. Crispy Chicken Drumettes

Crispy, flavorful chicken drumettes coated in a savory spice blend, perfect for a party or family snack.

Servings: 4
Preparation Time: 10 minutes
Cooking Time: 20 minutes
Ingredients:
- 2 lbs chicken drumettes (900 g)
- 2 tablespoons olive oil (30 ml)
- 1 teaspoon smoked paprika (5 g)
- 1 teaspoon garlic powder (5 g)
- 1/2 teaspoon onion powder (2.5 g)
- 1/2 teaspoon cayenne pepper (optional, 2.5 g)
- Salt and pepper to taste

Directions:
1. Preheat the Ninja Foodi to 400°F (200°C).
2. In a large bowl, toss the chicken drumettes with olive oil, smoked paprika, garlic powder, onion powder, cayenne pepper, salt, and pepper.
3. Place the drumettes in one basket and air fry for 20 minutes until golden and crispy, shaking the basket halfway through.
4. Serve hot with your favorite dipping sauce.

17. Mediterranean Chicken Wraps

Grilled chicken wrapped in a soft flatbread with fresh vegetables and a tangy yogurt sauce, perfect for a light and healthy meal.

Servings: 4
Preparation Time: 15 minutes
Cooking Time: 12 minutes
Ingredients:
- 1.5 lbs chicken breasts, sliced thinly (680 g)
- 2 tablespoons olive oil (30 ml)
- 1 teaspoon dried oregano (5 g)
- 1 teaspoon dried thyme (5 g)
- 1/2 teaspoon garlic powder (2.5 g)

- Salt and pepper to taste
- 4 flatbreads or pita breads
- Sliced tomatoes, cucumbers, red onions
- 1/2 cup plain Greek yogurt (120 ml)
- 1 tablespoon lemon juice (15 ml)
- 1 tablespoon fresh mint, chopped (optional, 5 g)

Directions:
1. Preheat the Ninja Foodi to 375°F (190°C).
2. In a large bowl, toss the chicken slices with olive oil, oregano, thyme, garlic powder, salt, and pepper.
3. Place the chicken in one basket and air fry for 10-12 minutes until cooked through, shaking the basket halfway through.
4. In a small bowl, mix Greek yogurt, lemon juice, and mint (if using) to make the sauce.
5. Assemble the wraps by placing the grilled chicken on the flatbread, adding sliced tomatoes, cucumbers, and red onions, and drizzling with the yogurt sauce. Wrap tightly and serve.

18. Parmesan-Crusted Turkey Cutlets

Turkey cutlets coated in a crispy Parmesan crust, air-fried to perfection and served with a lemon wedge.
Servings: 4
Preparation Time: 10 minutes
Cooking Time: 15 minutes
Ingredients:
- 1.5 lbs turkey cutlets (680 g)
- 1/2 cup all-purpose flour (60 g)
- 2 eggs, beaten
- 1 cup panko breadcrumbs (120 g)
- 1/2 cup grated Parmesan cheese (60 g)
- 1 teaspoon dried basil (5 g)
- 1 teaspoon garlic powder (5 g)
- Salt and pepper to taste
- Lemon wedges for serving

Directions:
1. Preheat the Ninja Foodi to 375°F (190°C).
2. Set up a breading station with three shallow dishes: one with flour, one with beaten eggs, and one with panko breadcrumbs mixed with

Parmesan cheese, basil, garlic powder, salt, and pepper.
3. Dredge each turkey cutlet in flour, dip in the egg, and then coat with the breadcrumb mixture.
4. Place the breaded cutlets in one basket and air fry for 12-15 minutes until golden and crispy, flipping halfway through.
5. Serve with lemon wedges and a side of steamed vegetables or a fresh salad.

19. Balsamic Glazed Chicken Thighs

Chicken thighs glazed with a rich and tangy balsamic reduction, creating a flavorful and elegant dish.
Servings: 4
Preparation Time: 10 minutes
Cooking Time: 25 minutes
Ingredients:
- 1.5 lbs chicken thighs, bone-in, skin-on (680 g)
- 1/4 cup balsamic vinegar (60 ml)
- 2 tablespoons honey (30 ml)
- 2 tablespoons olive oil (30 ml)
- 2 cloves garlic, minced
- Salt and pepper to taste
- Fresh rosemary for garnish (optional)

Directions:
1. Preheat the Ninja Foodi to 375°F (190°C).
2. In a small bowl, mix balsamic vinegar, honey, olive oil, garlic, salt, and pepper.
3. Brush the chicken thighs with the balsamic glaze, making sure to coat under the skin as well.
4. Place the chicken thighs in one basket, skin-side up, and air fry for 25 minutes until golden brown and cooked through, flipping halfway through.
5. Garnish with fresh rosemary and serve with mashed potatoes or roasted vegetables.

20. Chicken Fajitas

Juicy chicken strips seasoned with fajita spices and served with sautéed peppers and onions in warm tortillas.

Servings: 4
Preparation Time: 15 minutes
Cooking Time: 12 minutes
Ingredients:

- 1.5 lbs chicken breasts, sliced into strips (680 g)
- 1 tablespoon olive oil (15 ml)
- 1 teaspoon chili powder (5 g)
- 1 teaspoon cumin (5 g)
- 1/2 teaspoon smoked paprika (2.5 g)
- 1/2 teaspoon garlic powder (2.5 g)
- Salt and pepper to taste
- 1 red bell pepper, sliced
- 1 green bell pepper, sliced
- 1 onion, sliced
- 8 small flour tortillas

Directions:

1. Preheat the Ninja Foodi to 375°F (190°C).
2. In a large bowl, toss the chicken strips with olive oil, chili powder, cumin, smoked paprika, garlic powder, salt, and pepper.
3. Place the chicken in one basket and air fry for 8 minutes.
4. Add the sliced bell peppers and onion to the basket, toss with the chicken, and air fry for an additional 4 minutes until the vegetables are tender and the chicken is cooked through.
5. Serve the chicken and vegetables in warm tortillas with your favorite toppings like sour cream, guacamole, and salsa.

Chapter 13: Meat Lovers' Favorites

For those who crave hearty, protein-packed meals, this chapter is dedicated to you. The Ninja Foodi 2-Basket Air Fryer makes it easy to cook your favorite meats to perfection, whether you're grilling, roasting, or air frying. These ten recipes are designed to satisfy your cravings with rich flavors and tender textures, perfect for any meat lover.

1. Perfectly Grilled Ribeye Steak

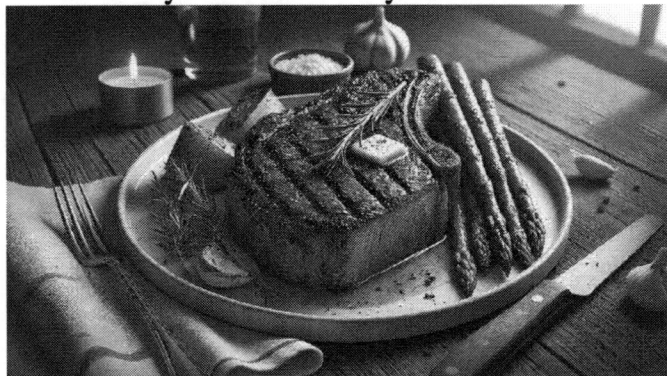

Juicy ribeye steaks seasoned with simple spices and grilled to your desired doneness, a classic and satisfying meal.

Servings: 2
Preparation Time: 10 minutes
Cooking Time: 12-15 minutes
Ingredients:

- 2 ribeye steaks, about 1 inch thick (approx. 12 oz each, 340 g)
- 2 tablespoons olive oil (30 ml)
- 1 teaspoon garlic powder (5 g)
- 1 teaspoon smoked paprika (5 g)
- 1/2 teaspoon salt (2.5 g)
- 1/2 teaspoon black pepper (2.5 g)

Directions:

1. Preheat the Ninja Foodi to 400°F (200°C).
2. Rub the steaks with olive oil, garlic powder, smoked paprika, salt, and pepper on both sides.
3. Place the steaks in one basket and air fry for 12-15 minutes, turning halfway through, until they reach your desired doneness (125°F/52°C for medium-rare).
4. Let the steaks rest for 5 minutes before serving. Pair with your favorite sides like mashed potatoes or a fresh salad.

2. BBQ Pork Ribs

Tender pork ribs slathered in smoky BBQ sauce and cooked to perfection, ideal for a weekend meal or a gathering.

Servings: 4
Preparation Time: 15 minutes (plus 2 hours for marinating)
Cooking Time: 30 minutes
Ingredients:

- 2 lbs pork ribs (900 g)
- 1/2 cup BBQ sauce (120 ml)
- 2 tablespoons brown sugar (30 g)
- 1 tablespoon smoked paprika (15 g)
- 1 teaspoon garlic powder (5 g)
- 1 teaspoon onion powder (5 g)
- 1/2 teaspoon cayenne pepper (2.5 g)
- Salt and pepper to taste

Directions:

1. In a small bowl, mix brown sugar, smoked paprika, garlic powder, onion powder, cayenne pepper, salt, and pepper. Rub the spice mixture all over the ribs.
2. Cover the ribs and refrigerate for at least 2 hours, preferably overnight.
3. Preheat the Ninja Foodi to 375°F (190°C).
4. Place the ribs in one basket and air fry for 25 minutes, flipping halfway through.

5. Brush the ribs with BBQ sauce and air fry for an additional 5 minutes until caramelized and sticky.
6. Serve with extra BBQ sauce and coleslaw.

3. Garlic Herb Lamb Chops

Succulent lamb chops marinated in garlic and herbs, then grilled to tender perfection, making for an elegant and flavorful dish.

Servings: 4
Preparation Time: 15 minutes (plus 1 hour for marinating)
Cooking Time: 12 minutes
Ingredients:
- 8 lamb chops (about 4 oz each, 115 g)
- 3 tablespoons olive oil (45 ml)
- 4 cloves garlic, minced
- 1 tablespoon fresh rosemary, chopped (5 g)
- 1 tablespoon fresh thyme, chopped (5 g)
- Juice of 1 lemon
- Salt and pepper to taste

Directions:
1. In a bowl, mix olive oil, garlic, rosemary, thyme, lemon juice, salt, and pepper. Rub the mixture all over the lamb chops and let them marinate for at least 1 hour.
2. Preheat the Ninja Foodi to 400°F (200°C).
3. Place the lamb chops in one basket and air fry for 10-12 minutes until they reach your desired doneness (145°F/63°C for medium-rare), flipping halfway through.
4. Let the lamb chops rest for a few minutes before serving with roasted vegetables or a side salad.

4. Juicy Bacon-Wrapped Meatloaf

A tender and juicy meatloaf wrapped in crispy bacon, offering a comforting and hearty meal that's sure to please.

Servings: 4
Preparation Time: 15 minutes
Cooking Time: 30 minutes
Ingredients:
- 1 lb ground beef (450 g)
- 1/2 lb ground pork (225 g)
- 1/2 cup breadcrumbs (60 g)
- 1 egg, beaten
- 1 small onion, finely chopped
- 2 cloves garlic, minced
- 1/4 cup ketchup (60 ml)
- 1 tablespoon Worcestershire sauce (15 ml)
- 8 slices bacon
- Salt and pepper to taste

Directions:
1. In a large bowl, mix ground beef, ground pork, breadcrumbs, egg, onion, garlic, ketchup, Worcestershire sauce, salt, and pepper until well combined.
2. Shape the mixture into a loaf and wrap it with bacon slices.
3. Preheat the Ninja Foodi to 375°F (190°C).
4. Place the meatloaf in one basket and air fry for 30 minutes until the bacon is crispy and the meatloaf is cooked through (160°F/71°C).
5. Let the meatloaf rest for a few minutes before slicing. Serve with mashed potatoes or green beans.

5. Korean BBQ Beef Skewers

Tender beef skewers marinated in a savory Korean BBQ sauce, grilled to perfection and served with rice or veggies.

Servings: 4
Preparation Time: 20 minutes (plus 2 hours for marinating)
Cooking Time: 10 minutes
Ingredients:
- 1.5 lbs beef sirloin, cut into 1-inch cubes (680 g)
- 1/4 cup soy sauce (60 ml)
- 2 tablespoons brown sugar (30 g)
- 2 tablespoons sesame oil (30 ml)
- 2 cloves garlic, minced
- 1 tablespoon grated fresh ginger (15 g)
- 1 tablespoon rice vinegar (15 ml)
- 1 teaspoon sesame seeds (optional, 5 g)
- Wooden or metal skewers

Directions:
1. In a large bowl, mix soy sauce, brown sugar, sesame oil, garlic, ginger, rice vinegar, and

sesame seeds (if using). Add the beef cubes and toss to coat. Cover and refrigerate for at least 2 hours, preferably overnight.

2. If using wooden skewers, soak them in water for 30 minutes to prevent burning. Thread the marinated beef cubes onto the skewers, leaving a little space between each piece.

3. Preheat the Ninja Foodi to 375°F (190°C). Grill the skewers for 8-10 minutes, turning occasionally, until the beef is cooked to your desired doneness.

4. Serve with steamed rice and sautéed vegetables.

6. Classic Beef Burgers

Juicy beef burgers cooked to perfection, served with all your favorite toppings for a satisfying and delicious meal.

Servings: 4
Preparation Time: 10 minutes
Cooking Time: 12 minutes
Ingredients:

- 1.5 lbs ground beef (80/20 blend) (680 g)
- 1 teaspoon garlic powder (5 g)
- 1 teaspoon onion powder (5 g)
- 1/2 teaspoon smoked paprika (2.5 g)
- Salt and pepper to taste
- 4 hamburger buns
- Toppings: lettuce, tomato, cheese, pickles, ketchup, mustard

Directions:

1. In a large bowl, mix ground beef with garlic powder, onion powder, smoked paprika, salt, and pepper. Form the mixture into four patties.

2. Preheat the Ninja Foodi to 375°F (190°C).

3. Place the burger patties in one basket and air fry for 10-12 minutes, flipping halfway through, until the burgers reach your desired doneness (160°F/71°C for medium).

4. Serve the burgers on buns with your favorite toppings.

7. Peppercorn-Crusted Filet Mignon

A luxurious filet mignon coated with crushed peppercorns and seared to perfection, creating a tender and flavorful dish.

Servings: 2
Preparation Time: 10 minutes
Cooking Time: 10-12 minutes
Ingredients:

- 2 filet mignon steaks (about 6 oz each, 170 g)
- 2 tablespoons olive oil (30 ml)
- 2 tablespoons crushed black peppercorns (30 g)
- 1 teaspoon garlic powder (5 g)
- Salt to taste

Directions:

1. Preheat the Ninja Foodi to 400°F (200°C).

2. Rub the steaks with olive oil, crushed peppercorns, garlic powder, and salt on both sides.

3. Place the steaks in one basket and air fry for 10-12 minutes, turning halfway through, until they reach your desired doneness (130°F/54°C for medium-rare).

4. Let the steaks rest for 5 minutes before serving. Pair with roasted potatoes or a green salad.

8. Spicy Italian Sausage with Peppers

Flavorful Italian sausages cooked with bell peppers and onions, offering a classic and hearty dish with a spicy kick.

Servings: 4
Preparation Time: 10 minutes
Cooking Time: 15 minutes
Ingredients:

- 4 spicy Italian sausages (about 12 oz, 340 g)
- 2 bell peppers, sliced
- 1 large onion, sliced
- 2 tablespoons olive oil (30 ml)
- 1 teaspoon garlic powder (5 g)
- 1 teaspoon dried oregano (5 g)
- Salt and pepper to taste

Directions:

1. Preheat the Ninja Foodi to 375°F (190°C).

2. Toss the bell peppers and onion with olive oil, garlic powder, oregano, salt, and pepper.

3. Place the sausages in one basket and the vegetables in the other. Air fry for 15 minutes, shaking the baskets halfway through, until the sausages are cooked through and the vegetables are tender.
4. Serve the sausages with the peppers and onions on a hoagie roll or alongside a salad.

9. Teriyaki Pork Tenderloin

Tender pork tenderloin marinated in a sweet and savory teriyaki sauce, air-fried to juicy perfection.

Servings: 4
Preparation Time: 15 minutes (plus 2 hours for marinating)
Cooking Time: 20 minutes
Ingredients:
- 1.5 lbs pork tenderloin (680 g)
- 1/4 cup soy sauce (60 ml)
- 2 tablespoons honey (30 ml)
- 1 tablespoon rice vinegar (15 ml)
- 1 tablespoon sesame oil (15 ml)
- 2 cloves garlic, minced
- 1 teaspoon grated fresh ginger (5 g)
- 1 tablespoon sesame seeds (optional, 15 g)

Directions:
1. In a small bowl, mix soy sauce, honey, rice vinegar, sesame oil, garlic, ginger, and sesame seeds (if using). Place the pork tenderloin in a resealable bag or a shallow dish and pour the marinade over it. Marinate in the refrigerator for at least 2 hours, preferably overnight.
2. Preheat the Ninja Foodi to 375°F (190°C).
3. Place the marinated pork tenderloin in one basket and air fry for 20 minutes, turning halfway through, until the internal temperature reaches 145°F (63°C).
4. Let the pork rest for 5 minutes before slicing. Serve with steamed rice and sautéed greens.

10. Bacon-Wrapped Filet Mignon

Filet mignon wrapped in crispy bacon, creating a rich and indulgent steakhouse-quality dish right at home.

Servings: 2
Preparation Time: 10 minutes
Cooking Time: 12-15 minutes

Ingredients:
- 2 filet mignon steaks (about 6 oz each, 170 g)
- 4 slices bacon
- 1 tablespoon olive oil (15 ml)
- 1 teaspoon garlic powder (5 g)
- 1 teaspoon dried thyme (5 g)
- Salt and pepper to taste
- Toothpicks for securing

Directions:
1. Preheat the Ninja Foodi to 400°F (200°C).
2. Rub the steaks with olive oil, garlic powder, thyme, salt, and pepper.
3. Wrap each steak with 2 slices of bacon, securing with toothpicks if necessary.
4. Place the bacon-wrapped steaks in one basket and air fry for 12-15 minutes, turning halfway through, until the steaks reach your desired doneness (130°F/54°C for medium-rare).
5. Let the steaks rest for 5 minutes before serving. Pair with mashed potatoes or steamed asparagus.

11. Rosemary-Garlic Roasted Lamb Shanks

Tender lamb shanks slow-cooked with rosemary, garlic, and a rich blend of spices, perfect for a hearty dinner.

Servings: 4
Preparation Time: 15 minutes
Cooking Time: 1 hour 30 minutes
Ingredients:
- 4 lamb shanks (about 1 lb each, 450 g)
- 3 tablespoons olive oil (45 ml)
- 4 cloves garlic, minced
- 2 tablespoons fresh rosemary, chopped (10 g)
- 1 teaspoon ground cumin (5 g)
- 1 teaspoon smoked paprika (5 g)
- Salt and pepper to taste
- 1 cup beef broth (240 ml)

Directions:
1. Preheat the Ninja Foodi to 350°F (175°C).
2. In a small bowl, mix olive oil, garlic, rosemary, cumin, smoked paprika, salt, and pepper. Rub the mixture all over the lamb shanks.
3. Place the lamb shanks in one basket and pour the beef broth around them.

4. Air fry for 1 hour and 30 minutes, turning halfway through, until the lamb is tender and cooked through.
5. Serve with mashed potatoes or a side of roasted vegetables.

12. Juicy Pork Chops with Apple Compote

Tender pork chops served with a sweet and tangy apple compote, making for a comforting and flavorful dish.

Servings: 4
Preparation Time: 10 minutes
Cooking Time: 20 minutes
Ingredients:
- 4 bone-in pork chops (about 8 oz each, 225 g)
- 2 tablespoons olive oil (30 ml)
- 1 teaspoon garlic powder (5 g)
- 1 teaspoon dried thyme (5 g)
- Salt and pepper to taste
- 2 apples, peeled, cored, and sliced
- 1/4 cup brown sugar (50 g)
- 1/2 teaspoon cinnamon (2.5 g)
- 1 tablespoon butter (15 g)

Directions:
1. Preheat the Ninja Foodi to 375°F (190°C).
2. Rub the pork chops with olive oil, garlic powder, thyme, salt, and pepper.
3. Place the pork chops in one basket and air fry for 15 minutes, turning halfway through, until cooked through.
4. In a small saucepan, melt butter over medium heat. Add the apples, brown sugar, and cinnamon. Cook for 5 minutes until the apples are tender.
5. Serve the pork chops with the warm apple compote.

13. Italian Meatball Subs

Hearty meatballs cooked in marinara sauce, served in a toasted sub roll with melted cheese, a perfect comfort food.

Servings: 4
Preparation Time: 15 minutes
Cooking Time: 20 minutes

Ingredients:
- 1 lb ground beef (450 g)
- 1/2 lb ground pork (225 g)
- 1/2 cup breadcrumbs (60 g)
- 1 egg, beaten
- 1/4 cup grated Parmesan cheese (30 g)
- 2 cloves garlic, minced
- 1 teaspoon dried oregano (5 g)
- Salt and pepper to taste
- 2 cups marinara sauce (480 ml)
- 4 sub rolls
- 1 cup shredded mozzarella cheese (120 g)

Directions:
1. In a large bowl, mix ground beef, ground pork, breadcrumbs, egg, Parmesan cheese, garlic, oregano, salt, and pepper until well combined. Form the mixture into meatballs.
2. Preheat the Ninja Foodi to 375°F (190°C).
3. Place the meatballs in one basket and air fry for 15 minutes until cooked through, shaking the basket halfway through.
4. Warm the marinara sauce in a saucepan. Add the meatballs to the sauce and simmer for 5 minutes.
5. Toast the sub rolls in the second basket for 2-3 minutes at 350°F (175°C).
6. Assemble the subs by placing the meatballs in the rolls, topping with sauce and shredded mozzarella cheese.

14. Beef and Mushroom Stroganoff

Tender beef strips cooked with mushrooms in a creamy sauce, served over egg noodles for a classic comfort dish.

Servings: 4
Preparation Time: 15 minutes
Cooking Time: 20 minutes
Ingredients:
- 1 lb beef sirloin, sliced into thin strips (450 g)
- 2 tablespoons olive oil (30 ml)
- 1 onion, chopped
- 2 cloves garlic, minced
- 8 oz mushrooms, sliced (225 g)
- 1 cup beef broth (240 ml)
- 1/2 cup sour cream (120 ml)
- 1 tablespoon Dijon mustard (15 g)

- Salt and pepper to taste
- 8 oz egg noodles, cooked (225 g)
- Fresh parsley, chopped (optional)

Directions:
1. Preheat the Ninja Foodi to 375°F (190°C).
2. In one basket, sauté the onion and garlic with olive oil until softened. Add the beef strips and cook until browned.
3. Add the mushrooms and cook for another 5 minutes until tender.
4. Stir in the beef broth, sour cream, and Dijon mustard. Simmer for 5 minutes until the sauce thickens.
5. Serve the stroganoff over cooked egg noodles, garnished with fresh parsley if desired.

15. Maple-Glazed Ham Steaks

Sweet and savory ham steaks glazed with a maple-brown sugar sauce, perfect for a quick and tasty dinner.

Servings: 4
Preparation Time: 5 minutes
Cooking Time: 10 minutes
Ingredients:
- 4 ham steaks (about 6 oz each, 170 g)
- 1/4 cup maple syrup (60 ml)
- 2 tablespoons brown sugar (30 g)
- 1 tablespoon Dijon mustard (15 g)
- 1 tablespoon apple cider vinegar (15 ml)
- 1/2 teaspoon ground cloves (2.5 g)

Directions:
1. Preheat the Ninja Foodi to 375°F (190°C).
2. In a small bowl, mix maple syrup, brown sugar, Dijon mustard, apple cider vinegar, and ground cloves.
3. Place the ham steaks in one basket and brush with the maple glaze.
4. Air fry for 8-10 minutes, flipping halfway through, until the glaze is caramelized and the ham is heated through.
5. Serve with roasted sweet potatoes or a fresh salad.

16. Cajun-Spiced Grilled Sausages

Spicy sausages grilled to perfection with Cajun seasoning, served with peppers and onions for a flavorful meal.

Servings: 4
Preparation Time: 10 minutes
Cooking Time: 15 minutes

Ingredients:
- 4 sausages (about 8 oz each, 225 g)
- 2 bell peppers, sliced
- 1 onion, sliced
- 2 tablespoons olive oil (30 ml)
- 1 tablespoon Cajun seasoning (15 g)
- Salt and pepper to taste

Directions:
1. Preheat the Ninja Foodi to 375°F (190°C).
2. Toss the bell peppers and onion with olive oil, Cajun seasoning, salt, and pepper.
3. Place the sausages in one basket and the vegetables in the other. Air fry for 15 minutes, shaking the baskets halfway through, until the sausages are cooked through and the vegetables are tender.
4. Serve the sausages with the peppers and onions on a roll or with rice.

17. Honey Garlic Glazed Chicken Drumsticks

Juicy chicken drumsticks coated in a sweet and sticky honey garlic glaze, perfect for a family-friendly meal.

Servings: 4
Preparation Time: 10 minutes
Cooking Time: 25 minutes
Ingredients:
- 2 lbs chicken drumsticks (900 g)
- 1/4 cup honey (60 ml)
- 2 tablespoons soy sauce (30 ml)
- 2 cloves garlic, minced
- 1 tablespoon olive oil (15 ml)
- 1 teaspoon ginger powder (5 g)
- Salt and pepper to taste

Directions:
1. Preheat the Ninja Foodi to 375°F (190°C).

2. In a small bowl, mix honey, soy sauce, garlic, olive oil, ginger powder, salt, and pepper.
3. Toss the chicken drumsticks in the honey garlic mixture.
4. Place the drumsticks in one basket and air fry for 25 minutes, flipping halfway through, until the chicken is cooked through and the glaze is caramelized.
5. Serve with steamed rice and a side of green beans.

18. Herb-Roasted Prime Rib

A show-stopping prime rib roast seasoned with herbs and garlic, cooked to perfection for a special occasion.

Servings: 6
Preparation Time: 15 minutes
Cooking Time: 1 hour 30 minutes
Ingredients:

- 4 lbs prime rib roast (1.8 kg)
- 4 cloves garlic, minced
- 2 tablespoons olive oil (30 ml)
- 2 tablespoons fresh rosemary, chopped (10 g)
- 2 tablespoons fresh thyme, chopped (10 g)
- 1 teaspoon black pepper (5 g)
- 1 teaspoon salt (5 g)

Directions:

1. Preheat the Ninja Foodi to 375°F (190°C).
2. In a small bowl, mix garlic, olive oil, rosemary, thyme, black pepper, and salt. Rub the mixture all over the prime rib.
3. Place the prime rib in one basket and air fry for 1 hour 30 minutes until the internal temperature reaches 130°F (54°C) for medium-rare, turning halfway through.
4. Let the prime rib rest for 15 minutes before carving. Serve with horseradish sauce and roasted potatoes.

19. Bourbon-Glazed Pork Tenderloin

Tender pork tenderloin glazed with a sweet and smoky bourbon sauce, making for a delicious and indulgent dish.

Servings: 4
Preparation Time: 10 minutes
Cooking Time: 20 minutes
Ingredients:

- 1.5 lbs pork tenderloin (680 g)
- 1/4 cup bourbon (60 ml)
- 1/4 cup brown sugar (50 g)
- 2 tablespoons soy sauce (30 ml)
- 1 tablespoon Dijon mustard (15 g)
- 2 cloves garlic, minced
- 1 tablespoon olive oil (15 ml)
- Salt and pepper to taste

Directions:

1. Preheat the Ninja Foodi to 375°F (190°C).
2. In a small bowl, mix bourbon, brown sugar, soy sauce, Dijon mustard, garlic, olive oil, salt, and pepper.
3. Brush the pork tenderloin with the bourbon glaze.
4. Place the tenderloin in one basket and air fry for 20 minutes, basting with more glaze halfway through, until the internal temperature reaches 145°F (63°C).
5. Let the pork rest for 5 minutes before slicing. Serve with mashed sweet potatoes or a side of sautéed greens.

20. Chimichurri Steak Fajitas

Juicy steak strips cooked with peppers and onions, topped with fresh chimichurri sauce for a flavorful and vibrant meal.

Servings: 4
Preparation Time: 20 minutes
Cooking Time: 15 minutes
Ingredients:

- 1.5 lbs flank steak, sliced into strips (680 g)
- 2 tablespoons olive oil (30 ml)
- 1 teaspoon chili powder (5 g)
- 1 teaspoon cumin (5 g)
- 1/2 teaspoon garlic powder (2.5 g)
- Salt and pepper to taste

- 2 bell peppers, sliced
- 1 onion, sliced
- 1/2 cup fresh chimichurri sauce (120 ml)
- 8 small flour tortillas

Directions:

1. Preheat the Ninja Foodi to 375°F (190°C).
2. Toss the steak strips with olive oil, chili powder, cumin, garlic powder, salt, and pepper.
3. Place the steak in one basket and air fry for 10 minutes.
4. Add the sliced bell peppers and onion to the basket, toss with the steak, and air fry for an additional 5 minutes until the vegetables are tender.
5. Serve the steak and vegetables in warm tortillas, topped with chimichurri sauce.

Chapter 14: Vegetarian and Plant-Based Delights

Embracing a plant-based diet doesn't mean sacrificing flavor. The Ninja Foodi 2-Basket Air Fryer makes it easy to create delicious, satisfying vegetarian dishes that everyone will love. Whether you're a full-time vegetarian or just looking to add more plant-based meals to your diet, these recipes offer a variety of tastes and textures that will delight your palate.

1. Crispy Cauliflower Buffalo Bites

Spicy and crispy cauliflower bites coated in buffalo sauce, perfect for a game day snack or a fun appetizer.

Servings: 4
Preparation Time: 15 minutes
Cooking Time: 15 minutes
Ingredients:
- 1 large head of cauliflower, cut into florets
- 1/2 cup all-purpose flour (60 g)
- 1/2 cup water (120 ml)
- 1/2 teaspoon garlic powder (2.5 g)
- 1/2 teaspoon onion powder (2.5 g)
- 1/2 cup buffalo sauce (120 ml)
- 1 tablespoon olive oil (15 ml)
- Salt and pepper to taste

Directions:
1. Preheat the Ninja Foodi to 375°F (190°C).
2. In a large bowl, mix flour, water, garlic powder, onion powder, salt, and pepper to create a batter.
3. Toss the cauliflower florets in the batter until fully coated.
4. Place the cauliflower in one basket and air fry for 12 minutes, shaking the basket halfway through.
5. In a separate bowl, mix buffalo sauce with olive oil. Toss the cooked cauliflower in the buffalo sauce.
6. Return the cauliflower to the basket and air fry for an additional 3 minutes. Serve with celery sticks and vegan ranch dressing.

2. Stuffed Portobello Mushrooms

Hearty Portobello mushrooms stuffed with a savory mixture of spinach, tomatoes, and cheese, offering a satisfying main dish or side.

Servings: 4
Preparation Time: 10 minutes
Cooking Time: 15 minutes
Ingredients:
- 4 large Portobello mushrooms, stems removed
- 2 cups fresh spinach, chopped (60 g)
- 1 cup cherry tomatoes, quartered (150 g)
- 1/2 cup shredded mozzarella cheese (120 g) (use vegan cheese for a plant-based option)
- 2 cloves garlic, minced
- 2 tablespoons olive oil (30 ml)
- Salt and pepper to taste

Directions:
1. Preheat the Ninja Foodi to 375°F (190°C).
2. Brush the mushroom caps with olive oil and season with salt and pepper.
3. In a bowl, mix spinach, cherry tomatoes, garlic, and mozzarella cheese.
4. Stuff the mushrooms with the spinach mixture and place them in one basket.
5. Air fry for 12-15 minutes until the mushrooms are tender and the cheese is melted.

6. Serve hot, garnished with fresh basil if desired.

3. Sweet Potato Fries with Avocado Dip

Crispy sweet potato fries served with a creamy and tangy avocado dip, perfect as a snack or side dish.

Servings: 4
Preparation Time: 10 minutes
Cooking Time: 20 minutes
Ingredients:

- 2 large sweet potatoes, cut into fries
- 2 tablespoons olive oil (30 ml)
- 1 teaspoon smoked paprika (5 g)
- 1/2 teaspoon garlic powder (2.5 g)
- Salt and pepper to taste
- 2 ripe avocados
- Juice of 1 lime
- 1 clove garlic, minced
- 2 tablespoons fresh cilantro, chopped (optional, 5 g)

Directions:

1. Preheat the Ninja Foodi to 400°F (200°C).
2. Toss the sweet potato fries with olive oil, smoked paprika, garlic powder, salt, and pepper.
3. Place the fries in one basket and air fry for 18-20 minutes until crispy, shaking the basket halfway through.
4. Meanwhile, in a bowl, mash the avocados and mix with lime juice, minced garlic, and cilantro.
5. Serve the sweet potato fries hot with the avocado dip.

4. Eggplant Parmesan

Layers of crispy eggplant, marinara sauce, and melted cheese, creating a comforting and satisfying vegetarian dish.

Servings: 4
Preparation Time: 15 minutes
Cooking Time: 20 minutes
Ingredients:

- 2 large eggplants, sliced into 1/2-inch rounds
- 1 cup panko breadcrumbs (120 g)
- 1/2 cup grated Parmesan cheese (60 g) (use nutritional yeast for a vegan option)
- 1 teaspoon dried oregano (5 g)
- 1 teaspoon garlic powder (5 g)
- 2 eggs, beaten (use flax eggs for a vegan option)
- 2 cups marinara sauce (480 ml)
- 1 cup shredded mozzarella cheese (120 g) (use vegan cheese for a plant-based option)
- Salt and pepper to taste

Directions:

1. Preheat the Ninja Foodi to 375°F (190°C).
2. In a bowl, mix panko breadcrumbs, Parmesan cheese, oregano, garlic powder, salt, and pepper.
3. Dip each eggplant slice into the beaten eggs, then coat with the breadcrumb mixture.
4. Place the breaded eggplant slices in one basket and air fry for 15 minutes until golden and crispy, flipping halfway through.
5. In a baking dish, layer the eggplant slices with marinara sauce and mozzarella cheese.
6. Air fry in the basket at 350°F (175°C) for an additional 5 minutes until the cheese is melted and bubbly. Serve hot.

5. Quinoa-Stuffed Bell Peppers

Colorful bell peppers stuffed with a flavorful mixture of quinoa, black beans, and corn, offering a complete and nutritious meal.

Servings: 4
Preparation Time: 20 minutes
Cooking Time: 15 minutes
Ingredients:

- 4 large bell peppers, tops cut off and seeds removed
- 1 cup cooked quinoa (185 g)
- 1 cup black beans, drained and rinsed (240 g)
- 1/2 cup corn kernels (120 g)
- 1/2 cup diced tomatoes (120 g)
- 1 teaspoon ground cumin (5 g)
- 1/2 teaspoon chili powder (2.5 g)
- 1/2 cup shredded cheddar cheese (120 g) (use vegan cheese for a plant-based option)
- Salt and pepper to taste

Directions:

1. Preheat the Ninja Foodi to 375°F (190°C).

2. In a bowl, mix cooked quinoa, black beans, corn, diced tomatoes, cumin, chili powder, salt, and pepper.
3. Stuff the bell peppers with the quinoa mixture and top with shredded cheddar cheese.
4. Place the stuffed peppers in one basket and air fry for 12-15 minutes until the peppers are tender and the cheese is melted.
5. Serve hot, garnished with fresh cilantro if desired.

6. Tofu Stir-Fry with Vegetables

Crispy tofu stir-fried with colorful vegetables in a savory sauce, offering a quick and healthy plant-based meal.

Servings: 4
Preparation Time: 15 minutes
Cooking Time: 15 minutes
Ingredients:

- 1 block firm tofu, pressed and cubed (about 14 oz, 400 g)
- 2 tablespoons soy sauce (30 ml)
- 1 tablespoon sesame oil (15 ml)
- 1 tablespoon cornstarch (15 g)
- 1 red bell pepper, sliced
- 1 yellow bell pepper, sliced
- 1 zucchini, sliced
- 1 carrot, julienned
- 2 cloves garlic, minced
- 2 tablespoons stir-fry sauce (30 ml)

Directions:

1. Preheat the Ninja Foodi to 375°F (190°C).
2. Toss the tofu cubes with soy sauce, sesame oil, and cornstarch.
3. Place the tofu in one basket and air fry for 10 minutes until crispy, shaking the basket halfway through.
4. Add the vegetables and garlic to the basket, toss with the tofu, and air fry for an additional 5 minutes until the vegetables are tender.
5. Drizzle with stir-fry sauce and serve over rice or noodles.

7. Zucchini Noodles with Pesto

Light and healthy zucchini noodles tossed with fresh pesto, creating a low-carb, flavorful dish.

Servings: 4
Preparation Time: 10 minutes
Cooking Time: 5 minutes
Ingredients:

- 4 medium zucchinis, spiralized into noodles
- 1/2 cup basil pesto (120 g)
- 1/4 cup cherry tomatoes, halved (60 g)
- 1/4 cup grated Parmesan cheese (30 g) (use nutritional yeast for a vegan option)
- 1 tablespoon olive oil (15 ml)
- Salt and pepper to taste

Directions:

1. Preheat the Ninja Foodi to 350°F (175°C).
2. Toss the zucchini noodles with olive oil, salt, and pepper.
3. Place the zucchini noodles in one basket and air fry for 3-5 minutes until just tender.
4. Remove the noodles and toss with pesto, cherry tomatoes, and Parmesan cheese.
5. Serve immediately, garnished with fresh basil if desired.

8. Baked Falafel with Tahini Sauce

Crispy baked falafel served with a creamy tahini sauce, offering a delicious and nutritious plant-based meal.

Servings: 4
Preparation Time: 15 minutes (plus 30 minutes for chilling)
Cooking Time: 15 minutes
Ingredients:

- 1 can chickpeas, drained and rinsed (15 oz, 425 g)
- 1/4 cup fresh parsley, chopped (15 g)
- 1/4 cup fresh cilantro, chopped (15 g)
- 1 small onion, chopped
- 2 cloves garlic, minced
- 1 teaspoon ground cumin (5 g)
- 1 teaspoon ground coriander (5 g)
- 1/2 teaspoon baking powder (2.5 g)
- 2 tablespoons all-purpose flour (30 g)
- Salt and pepper to taste
- Olive oil spray

- 1/4 cup tahini (60 g)
- 2 tablespoons lemon juice (30 ml)
- 1 clove garlic, minced
- 2 tablespoons water (30 ml)

Directions:

1. In a food processor, combine chickpeas, parsley, cilantro, onion, garlic, cumin, coriander, baking powder, flour, salt, and pepper. Pulse until the mixture is well combined but still slightly chunky.
2. Form the mixture into small patties and chill in the refrigerator for 30 minutes.
3. Preheat the Ninja Foodi to 375°F (190°C).
4. Place the falafel patties in one basket, spray with olive oil, and air fry for 12-15 minutes until golden and crispy, flipping halfway through.
5. In a small bowl, mix tahini, lemon juice, garlic, and water to make the sauce.
6. Serve the falafel with the tahini sauce and a side of pita bread or salad.

9. Spinach and Feta Stuffed Peppers

Bell peppers stuffed with a mixture of spinach, feta and quinoa, creating a flavorful and filling vegetarian dish.

Servings: 4
Preparation Time: 15 minutes
Cooking Time: 15 minutes
Ingredients:

- 4 large bell peppers, tops cut off and seeds removed
- 1 cup cooked quinoa (185 g)
- 2 cups fresh spinach, chopped (60 g)
- 1/2 cup crumbled feta cheese (120 g) (use vegan feta for a plant-based option)
- 1/4 cup sun-dried tomatoes, chopped (30 g)
- 1 clove garlic, minced
- 1 tablespoon olive oil (15 ml)
- Salt and pepper to taste

Directions:

1. Preheat the Ninja Foodi to 375°F (190°C).
2. In a bowl, mix cooked quinoa, spinach, feta, sun-dried tomatoes, garlic, olive oil, salt, and pepper.

3. Stuff the bell peppers with the quinoa mixture and place them in one basket.
4. Air fry for 12-15 minutes until the peppers are tender and the filling is heated through.
5. Serve hot, garnished with fresh parsley if desired.

10. Crispy Avocado Tacos

Crispy avocado slices served in soft tortillas with fresh salsa and a creamy lime sauce, perfect for a light and flavorful meal.

Servings: 4
Preparation Time: 15 minutes
Cooking Time: 10 minutes
Ingredients:

- 2 ripe avocados, sliced
- 1/2 cup panko breadcrumbs (60 g)
- 1/4 cup all-purpose flour (30 g)
- 1 egg, beaten (use flax egg for a vegan option)
- Salt and pepper to taste
- 8 small flour tortillas
- 1 cup shredded lettuce (60 g)
- 1/2 cup salsa (120 ml)
- 1/4 cup sour cream (60 g) (use vegan sour cream for a plant-based option)
- 1 tablespoon lime juice (15 ml)

Directions:

1. Preheat the Ninja Foodi to 375°F (190°C).
2. Set up a breading station with three shallow dishes: one with flour, one with beaten egg, and one with panko breadcrumbs seasoned with salt and pepper.
3. Dredge each avocado slice in flour, dip in the egg, and then coat with the breadcrumbs.
4. Place the avocado slices in one basket and air fry for 8-10 minutes until golden and crispy, shaking the basket halfway through.
5. In a small bowl, mix sour cream with lime juice.
6. Serve the crispy avocado in tortillas with shredded lettuce, salsa, and a drizzle of lime sour cream.

11. Cauliflower Tacos with Chipotle Lime Sauce

Roasted cauliflower florets seasoned with spices and served in warm tortillas with a tangy chipotle lime sauce.

Servings: 4
Preparation Time: 15 minutes
Cooking Time: 20 minutes
Ingredients:

- 1 large head of cauliflower, cut into florets
- 2 tablespoons olive oil (30 ml)
- 1 teaspoon smoked paprika (5 g)
- 1 teaspoon ground cumin (5 g)
- 1/2 teaspoon garlic powder (2.5 g)
- Salt and pepper to taste
- 8 small corn tortillas
- 1/2 cup shredded cabbage (60 g)
- 1/4 cup vegan mayonnaise (60 g)
- 1 tablespoon chipotle in adobo sauce, minced (15 ml)
- 1 tablespoon lime juice (15 ml)
- Fresh cilantro for garnish

Directions:

1. Preheat the Ninja Foodi to 375°F (190°C).
2. Toss the cauliflower florets with olive oil, smoked paprika, cumin, garlic powder, salt, and pepper.
3. Place the cauliflower in one basket and air fry for 15-20 minutes until tender and slightly crispy, shaking the basket halfway through.
4. In a small bowl, mix vegan mayonnaise, chipotle, and lime juice to make the sauce.
5. Warm the tortillas in the second basket for 2-3 minutes at 350°F (175°C).
6. Assemble the tacos by placing roasted cauliflower in each tortilla, topping with shredded cabbage, a drizzle of chipotle lime sauce, and fresh cilantro.

12. Lentil and Veggie Burgers

Hearty lentil burgers packed with vegetables and spices, served on a bun with your favorite toppings.

Servings: 4
Preparation Time: 20 minutes
Cooking Time: 15 minutes

Ingredients:

- 1 cup cooked lentils (200 g)
- 1/2 cup grated carrot (60 g)
- 1/2 cup grated zucchini (60 g)
- 1/4 cup breadcrumbs (30 g)
- 1/4 cup chopped onion (30 g)
- 1 clove garlic, minced
- 1 tablespoon soy sauce (15 ml)
- 1 teaspoon smoked paprika (5 g)
- 1/2 teaspoon ground cumin (2.5 g)
- Salt and pepper to taste
- Olive oil spray
- 4 hamburger buns
- Toppings: lettuce, tomato, avocado, vegan mayo

Directions:

1. Preheat the Ninja Foodi to 375°F (190°C).
2. In a large bowl, mash the lentils and mix in grated carrot, zucchini, breadcrumbs, onion, garlic, soy sauce, smoked paprika, cumin, salt, and pepper.
3. Form the mixture into patties and spray with olive oil.
4. Place the patties in one basket and air fry for 12-15 minutes until golden and firm, flipping halfway through.
5. Serve on buns with your favorite toppings.

13. Mediterranean Quinoa Salad

A refreshing quinoa salad with cucumbers, tomatoes, olives, and feta, tossed in a lemony vinaigrette.

Servings: 4
Preparation Time: 15 minutes
Cooking Time: 10 minutes (for cooking quinoa)
Ingredients:

- 1 cup cooked quinoa (185 g)
- 1 cup diced cucumber (120 g)
- 1 cup cherry tomatoes, halved (150 g)
- 1/2 cup Kalamata olives, pitted and halved (75 g)
- 1/4 cup crumbled feta cheese (60 g) (use vegan feta for a plant-based option)
- 1/4 cup red onion, finely chopped (30 g)
- 2 tablespoons olive oil (30 ml)
- 1 tablespoon lemon juice (15 ml)

- 1 teaspoon dried oregano (5 g)
- Salt and pepper to taste

Directions:
1. In a large bowl, combine cooked quinoa, cucumber, cherry tomatoes, olives, feta cheese, and red onion.
2. In a small bowl, whisk together olive oil, lemon juice, oregano, salt, and pepper.
3. Pour the dressing over the quinoa salad and toss to combine.
4. Serve chilled or at room temperature.

14. Grilled Vegetable Skewers

Colorful vegetable skewers grilled to perfection, served with a tangy balsamic glaze.

Servings: 4
Preparation Time: 15 minutes
Cooking Time: 12 minutes
Ingredients:
- 1 zucchini, sliced into rounds
- 1 yellow squash, sliced into rounds
- 1 red bell pepper, cut into chunks
- 1 red onion, cut into chunks
- 8 cherry tomatoes
- 2 tablespoons olive oil (30 ml)
- Salt and pepper to taste
- 2 tablespoons balsamic vinegar (30 ml)
- 1 tablespoon honey (15 ml) (or maple syrup for vegan)

Directions:
1. Preheat the Ninja Foodi to 375°F (190°C).
2. Toss the vegetables with olive oil, salt, and pepper.
3. Thread the vegetables onto skewers.
4. Place the skewers in one basket and air fry for 10-12 minutes until tender and slightly charred, turning halfway through.
5. In a small bowl, mix balsamic vinegar and honey. Brush the skewers with the balsamic glaze before serving.

15. Spinach and Artichoke Stuffed Mushrooms

Portobello mushrooms stuffed with a creamy spinach and artichoke filling, baked to perfection.

Servings: 4
Preparation Time: 15 minutes
Cooking Time: 15 minutes
Ingredients:
- 4 large Portobello mushrooms, stems removed
- 1 cup fresh spinach, chopped (30 g)
- 1/2 cup canned artichoke hearts, chopped (75 g)
- 1/4 cup vegan cream cheese (60 g)
- 2 tablespoons nutritional yeast (15 g)
- 2 cloves garlic, minced
- Salt and pepper to taste
- Olive oil spray

Directions:
1. Preheat the Ninja Foodi to 375°F (190°C).
2. In a bowl, mix spinach, artichoke hearts, vegan cream cheese, nutritional yeast, garlic, salt, and pepper.
3. Stuff the mushrooms with the spinach mixture and spray lightly with olive oil.
4. Place the stuffed mushrooms in one basket and air fry for 12-15 minutes until the mushrooms are tender and the filling is golden.
5. Serve as an appetizer or a side dish.

16. Vegan Stuffed Acorn Squash

Roasted acorn squash stuffed with a savory mix of quinoa, cranberries, and pecans, perfect for a holiday meal.

Servings: 4
Preparation Time: 15 minutes
Cooking Time: 25 minutes
Ingredients:
- 2 acorn squashes, halved and seeded
- 1 cup cooked quinoa (185 g)
- 1/4 cup dried cranberries (30 g)
- 1/4 cup chopped pecans (30 g)
- 1 tablespoon maple syrup (15 ml)
- 1 teaspoon ground cinnamon (5 g)
- 1/2 teaspoon ground nutmeg (2.5 g)
- 1 tablespoon olive oil (15 ml)

- Salt and pepper to taste

Directions:
1. Preheat the Ninja Foodi to 375°F (190°C).
2. Brush the cut sides of the acorn squash with olive oil and season with salt and pepper.
3. Place the squash halves cut-side down in one basket and air fry for 20 minutes until tender.
4. In a bowl, mix cooked quinoa, cranberries, pecans, maple syrup, cinnamon, nutmeg, salt, and pepper.
5. Flip the squash halves over, stuff with the quinoa mixture, and air fry for an additional 5 minutes.
6. Serve hot, garnished with fresh herbs if desired.

17. Thai Peanut Noodles

Rice noodles tossed in a creamy peanut sauce with fresh vegetables, creating a flavorful and satisfying dish.

Servings: 4
Preparation Time: 10 minutes
Cooking Time: 10 minutes
Ingredients:
- 8 oz rice noodles (225 g)
- 1/4 cup peanut butter (60 g)
- 2 tablespoons soy sauce (30 ml)
- 1 tablespoon rice vinegar (15 ml)
- 1 tablespoon lime juice (15 ml)
- 1 tablespoon maple syrup (15 ml)
- 1 clove garlic, minced
- 1/2 teaspoon sriracha (optional, 2.5 ml)
- 1 red bell pepper, sliced
- 1 carrot, julienned
- 1/4 cup chopped peanuts (30 g)
- Fresh cilantro for garnish

Directions:
1. Cook the rice noodles according to package instructions. Drain and set aside.
2. In a small saucepan, combine peanut butter, soy sauce, rice vinegar, lime juice, maple syrup, garlic, and sriracha. Cook over low heat until smooth and well combined.
3. Toss the cooked noodles with the peanut sauce and add the bell pepper and carrot.
4. Serve topped with chopped peanuts and fresh cilantro.

18. Vegan Shepherd's Pie

A hearty vegan version of shepherd's pie, made with lentils, vegetables, and topped with creamy mashed potatoes.

Servings: 4
Preparation Time: 20 minutes
Cooking Time: 25 minutes
Ingredients:
- 1 cup cooked lentils (200 g)
- 1 onion, chopped
- 2 cloves garlic, minced
- 2 carrots, diced
- 1/2 cup frozen peas (75 g)
- 1/2 cup vegetable broth (120 ml)
- 2 tablespoons tomato paste (30 g)
- 1 teaspoon dried thyme (5 g)
- 1 teaspoon dried rosemary (5 g)
- Salt and pepper to taste
- 4 cups mashed potatoes (960 g) (use plant-based milk and butter for vegan)
- Olive oil spray

Directions:
1. Preheat the Ninja Foodi to 375°F (190°C).
2. In a skillet, sauté onion and garlic until softened. Add carrots and cook for 5 minutes.
3. Stir in cooked lentils, peas, vegetable broth, tomato paste, thyme, rosemary, salt, and pepper. Cook for another 5 minutes.
4. Transfer the lentil mixture to a baking dish and top with mashed potatoes.
5. Spray the top with olive oil and place in one basket. Air fry for 15-20 minutes until the top is golden and crispy.
6. Serve hot, garnished with fresh herbs if desired.

19. Balsamic Glazed Brussels Sprouts

Crispy Brussels sprouts tossed in a sweet and tangy balsamic glaze, perfect as a side dish or snack.

Servings: 4
Preparation Time: 10 minutes
Cooking Time: 15 minutes
Ingredients:
- 1 lb Brussels sprouts, trimmed and halved (450 g)
- 2 tablespoons olive oil (30 ml)

- 2 tablespoons balsamic vinegar (30 ml)
- 1 tablespoon maple syrup (15 ml)
- 1 teaspoon Dijon mustard (5 g)
- Salt and pepper to taste

Directions:
1. Preheat the Ninja Foodi to 375°F (190°C).
2. Toss the Brussels sprouts with olive oil, salt, and pepper.
3. Place the Brussels sprouts in one basket and air fry for 12-15 minutes until crispy, shaking the basket halfway through.
4. In a small bowl, whisk together balsamic vinegar, maple syrup, and Dijon mustard.
5. Toss the cooked Brussels sprouts in the balsamic glaze and serve hot.

20. Ratatouille

A classic French vegetable dish featuring a medley of roasted eggplant, zucchini, bell peppers, and tomatoes, seasoned with herbs.

Servings: 4
Preparation Time: 15 minutes
Cooking Time: 25 minutes
Ingredients:
- 1 eggplant, diced
- 1 zucchini, sliced
- 1 yellow squash, sliced
- 1 red bell pepper, diced
- 1 onion, sliced
- 2 cloves garlic, minced
- 2 tablespoons olive oil (30 ml)
- 1 teaspoon dried thyme (5 g)
- 1 teaspoon dried basil (5 g)
- Salt and pepper to taste
- 1 cup tomato sauce (240 ml)

Directions:
1. Preheat the Ninja Foodi to 375°F (190°C).
2. Toss the eggplant, zucchini, yellow squash, red bell pepper, onion, and garlic with olive oil, thyme, basil, salt, and pepper.
3. Place the vegetables in one basket and air fry for 20 minutes until tender, shaking the basket halfway through.
4. Serve the roasted vegetables over warm tomato sauce, garnished with fresh basil if desired.

Chapter 15: Easy Weeknight Meals

When the workday winds down and hunger sets in, you want meals that are quick, easy, and still packed with flavor. With the Ninja Foodi 2-Basket Air Fryer, preparing dinner on busy weeknights becomes a breeze. These ten recipes are designed to be both simple and delicious, allowing you to whip up a nutritious meal in no time, without sacrificing taste.

1. Lemon Garlic Chicken Thighs

Juicy chicken thighs marinated in a zesty lemon garlic sauce, then air-fried to golden perfection.

Servings: 4

Preparation Time: 10 minutes (plus 30 minutes for marinating)

Cooking Time: 20 minutes

Ingredients:

- 1.5 lbs chicken thighs, bone-in, skin-on (680 g)
- 1/4 cup olive oil (60 ml)
- Juice of 1 lemon
- 3 cloves garlic, minced
- 1 teaspoon dried oregano (5 g)
- 1/2 teaspoon salt (2.5 g)
- 1/2 teaspoon black pepper (2.5 g)

Directions:

1. In a large bowl, combine olive oil, lemon juice, minced garlic, oregano, salt, and pepper. Add the chicken thighs and toss to coat. Marinate for at least 30 minutes.
2. Preheat the Ninja Foodi to 375°F (190°C).
3. Place the marinated chicken thighs in one basket, skin-side up, and air fry for 20 minutes until the chicken is golden brown and cooked through, flipping halfway through.
4. Serve with a side of steamed vegetables or roasted potatoes for a complete meal.

2. Honey Mustard Salmon

Tender salmon fillets glazed with a sweet and tangy honey mustard sauce, perfect for a light and healthy dinner.

Servings: 4

Preparation Time: 5 minutes

Cooking Time: 12 minutes

Ingredients:

- 4 salmon fillets (about 6 oz each, 170 g)
- 2 tablespoons honey (30 ml)
- 2 tablespoons Dijon mustard (30 g)
- 1 tablespoon olive oil (15 ml)
- 1 teaspoon dried thyme (5 g)
- Salt and pepper to taste

Directions:

1. Preheat the Ninja Foodi to 375°F (190°C).
2. In a small bowl, whisk together honey, Dijon mustard, olive oil, thyme, salt, and pepper.
3. Brush the salmon fillets with the honey mustard glaze.
4. Place the salmon fillets in one basket and air fry for 10-12 minutes until the salmon is cooked through and flaky.
5. Serve with a fresh salad or steamed asparagus for a healthy, quick meal.

3. Quick Beef Stir-Fry

Thin slices of beef and colorful vegetables cooked in a savory sauce, served over rice for a satisfying dinner.

Servings: 4

Preparation Time: 10 minutes

Cooking Time: 15 minutes

Ingredients:

- 1 lb beef sirloin, thinly sliced (450 g)
- 1 red bell pepper, sliced
- 1 green bell pepper, sliced
- 1 onion, sliced
- 2 cloves garlic, minced
- 2 tablespoons soy sauce (30 ml)
- 1 tablespoon oyster sauce (15 ml)
- 1 tablespoon sesame oil (15 ml)
- 1 teaspoon cornstarch (5 g)
- Cooked rice for serving

Directions:

1. Preheat the Ninja Foodi to 375°F (190°C).
2. In a bowl, toss the beef slices with soy sauce, oyster sauce, sesame oil, garlic, and cornstarch.
3. Place the beef in one basket and the sliced vegetables in the other. Air fry for 10 minutes, shaking the baskets halfway through.
4. Combine the beef and vegetables and air fry for an additional 5 minutes.
5. Serve over cooked rice and enjoy a quick, flavorful meal.

4. BBQ Chicken Drumsticks

Flavorful chicken drumsticks coated in a tangy BBQ sauce, perfect for a crowd-pleasing weeknight dinner.

Servings: 4

Preparation Time: 5 minutes

Cooking Time: 25 minutes

Ingredients:

- 2 lbs chicken drumsticks (900 g)
- 1/2 cup BBQ sauce (120 ml)
- 1 tablespoon olive oil (15 ml)
- 1 teaspoon smoked paprika (5 g)
- Salt and pepper to taste

Directions:

1. Preheat the Ninja Foodi to 375°F (190°C).
2. Toss the chicken drumsticks with olive oil, smoked paprika, salt, and pepper.
3. Place the drumsticks in one basket and air fry for 20 minutes, flipping halfway through.
4. Brush the drumsticks with BBQ sauce and air fry for an additional 5 minutes until the sauce is caramelized.
5. Serve with coleslaw or corn on the cob for a classic meal.

5. Shrimp Scampi

Succulent shrimp cooked in a garlic butter sauce, served over pasta or with crusty bread for a delicious dinner.

Servings: 4

Preparation Time: 10 minutes

Cooking Time: 10 minutes

Ingredients:

- 1 lb large shrimp, peeled and deveined (450 g)
- 4 tablespoons butter, melted (60 g)
- 3 cloves garlic, minced
- Juice of 1 lemon
- 1/4 cup white wine (60 ml) (optional)
- 1 tablespoon chopped parsley (5 g)
- Salt and pepper to taste

Directions:

1. Preheat the Ninja Foodi to 375°F (190°C).
2. In a bowl, toss the shrimp with melted butter, garlic, lemon juice, white wine (if using), salt, and pepper.
3. Place the shrimp in one basket and air fry for 8-10 minutes until the shrimp are pink and cooked through, shaking the basket halfway through.
4. Garnish with chopped parsley and serve over pasta or with crusty bread.

6. Vegetarian Stuffed Peppers

Bell peppers stuffed with a savory mixture of quinoa, black beans, and vegetables, making a nutritious and filling dinner.

Servings: 4

Preparation Time: 15 minutes

Cooking Time: 15 minutes

Ingredients:

- 4 large bell peppers, tops cut off and seeds removed
- 1 cup cooked quinoa (185 g)

- 1 cup black beans, drained and rinsed (240 g)
- 1/2 cup corn kernels (120 g)
- 1/2 cup diced tomatoes (120 g)
- 1 teaspoon ground cumin (5 g)
- 1/2 teaspoon chili powder (2.5 g)
- 1/2 cup shredded cheddar cheese (120 g) (use vegan cheese for a plant-based option)
- Salt and pepper to taste

Directions:
1. Preheat the Ninja Foodi to 375°F (190°C).
2. In a bowl, mix cooked quinoa, black beans, corn, diced tomatoes, cumin, chili powder, salt, and pepper.
3. Stuff the bell peppers with the quinoa mixture and top with shredded cheddar cheese.
4. Place the stuffed peppers in one basket and air fry for 12-15 minutes until the peppers are tender and the cheese is melted.
5. Serve with a side salad or guacamole.

7. Teriyaki Chicken Skewers

Juicy chicken skewers marinated in a savory teriyaki sauce, grilled to perfection for a quick and delicious meal.

Servings: 4
Preparation Time: 15 minutes (plus 30 minutes for marinating)
Cooking Time: 15 minutes
Ingredients:
- 1.5 lbs chicken breast, cut into 1-inch cubes (680 g)
- 1/4 cup soy sauce (60 ml)
- 2 tablespoons honey (30 ml)
- 2 tablespoons rice vinegar (30 ml)
- 1 tablespoon sesame oil (15 ml)
- 2 cloves garlic, minced
- 1 teaspoon grated fresh ginger (5 g)
- Wooden or metal skewers

Directions:
1. In a large bowl, combine soy sauce, honey, rice vinegar, sesame oil, garlic, and ginger. Add the chicken cubes and mix well to coat. Marinate for at least 30 minutes.
2. Preheat the Ninja Foodi to 375°F (190°C).

3. Thread the marinated chicken cubes onto the skewers, leaving a little space between each piece.
4. Place the skewers in one basket and air fry for 12-15 minutes, turning occasionally, until the chicken is fully cooked.
5. Serve with steamed rice and stir-fried vegetables.

8. Baked Ziti

A comforting dish of baked pasta with marinara sauce and melted cheese, perfect for a quick and easy weeknight meal.

Servings: 4
Preparation Time: 10 minutes
Cooking Time: 20 minutes
Ingredients:
- 8 oz ziti pasta (225 g)
- 2 cups marinara sauce (480 ml)
- 1 cup ricotta cheese (250 g)
- 1/2 cup shredded mozzarella cheese (120 g)
- 1/4 cup grated Parmesan cheese (30 g)
- 1 teaspoon dried basil (5 g)
- 1 teaspoon dried oregano (5 g)
- Salt and pepper to taste

Directions:
1. Preheat the Ninja Foodi to 375°F (190°C).
2. Cook the ziti pasta according to package instructions. Drain and set aside.
3. In a large bowl, mix the cooked ziti with marinara sauce, ricotta cheese, basil, oregano, salt, and pepper.
4. Transfer the mixture to a baking dish, sprinkle with mozzarella and Parmesan cheese, and place the dish in one basket.
5. Air fry for 15-20 minutes until the cheese is melted and bubbly.
6. Serve hot with garlic bread or a side salad.

9. Garlic Butter Shrimp and Asparagus

A quick and flavorful dish of shrimp and asparagus cooked in a garlic butter sauce, perfect for a light and satisfying meal.

Servings: 4

Preparation Time: 10 minutes

Cooking Time: 10 minutes

Ingredients:

- 1 lb large shrimp, peeled and deveined (450 g)
- 1 bunch asparagus, trimmed and cut into 2-inch pieces
- 4 tablespoons butter, melted (60 g)
- 3 cloves garlic, minced
- Juice of 1 lemon
- Salt and pepper to taste

Directions:

1. Preheat the Ninja Foodi to 375°F (190°C).
2. In a bowl, toss the shrimp and asparagus with melted butter, garlic, lemon juice, salt, and pepper.
3. Place the shrimp and asparagus in one basket and air fry for 8-10 minutes until the shrimp are pink and the asparagus is tender, shaking the basket halfway through.
4. Serve hot with a side of rice or crusty bread.

10. Spinach and Mushroom Quesadillas

Crispy quesadillas filled with sautéed spinach, mushrooms, and melted cheese, perfect for a quick and easy dinner.

Servings: 4

Preparation Time: 10 minutes

Cooking Time: 10 minutes

Ingredients:

- 4 large flour tortillas
- 2 cups fresh spinach, chopped (60 g)
- 1 cup sliced mushrooms (100 g)
- 1 cup shredded cheddar cheese (120 g) (use vegan cheese for a plant-based option)
- 1 tablespoon olive oil (15 ml)
- Salt and pepper to taste

Directions:

1. Preheat the Ninja Foodi to 375°F (190°C).
2. In a skillet, sauté the spinach and mushrooms with olive oil, salt, and pepper until the vegetables are softened.
3. Place a tortilla on a flat surface and sprinkle half of it with shredded cheese, spinach, and mushrooms. Fold the tortilla in half to cover the filling.
4. Spray the quesadilla lightly with olive oil and place it in one basket. Air fry for 5 minutes on each side until golden and crispy.
5. Slice into wedges and serve with salsa, guacamole, or sour cream.

11. Margherita Flatbread Pizza

A simple and delicious flatbread pizza topped with fresh tomatoes, mozzarella, and basil for a quick weeknight dinner.

Servings: 4

Preparation Time: 10 minutes

Cooking Time: 12 minutes

Ingredients:

- 2 large flatbreads
- 1/2 cup marinara sauce (120 ml)
- 1 cup shredded mozzarella cheese (120 g)
- 1 large tomato, thinly sliced
- 1/4 cup fresh basil leaves
- 1 tablespoon olive oil (15 ml)
- Salt and pepper to taste

Directions:

1. Preheat the Ninja Foodi to 375°F (190°C).
2. Spread the marinara sauce evenly over the flatbreads.
3. Top with shredded mozzarella, sliced tomatoes, salt, and pepper.
4. Place the flatbreads in one basket and air fry for 10-12 minutes until the cheese is melted and bubbly.
5. Remove from the air fryer and garnish with fresh basil leaves and a drizzle of olive oil before serving.

12. Spaghetti Aglio e Olio

A quick and easy pasta dish made with garlic, olive oil, red pepper flakes, and Parmesan cheese.

Servings: 4

Preparation Time: 5 minutes

Cooking Time: 15 minutes

Ingredients:

- 12 oz spaghetti (340 g)
- 1/4 cup olive oil (60 ml)
- 6 cloves garlic, thinly sliced
- 1/2 teaspoon red pepper flakes (2.5 g)
- 1/4 cup grated Parmesan cheese (30 g) (use vegan Parmesan for a plant-based option)
- 1/4 cup fresh parsley, chopped (15 g)
- Salt and pepper to taste

Directions:

1. Cook the spaghetti according to package instructions. Drain and set aside.
2. In a skillet, heat olive oil over medium heat and sauté garlic until golden and fragrant.
3. Add red pepper flakes, salt, and pepper, and cook for another minute.
4. Toss the cooked spaghetti in the garlic oil and top with grated Parmesan cheese and fresh parsley.
5. Serve immediately with a side of crusty bread.

13. BBQ Pulled Jackfruit Sandwiches

A delicious plant-based alternative to pulled pork, using jackfruit cooked in BBQ sauce and served on soft buns.

Servings: 4

Preparation Time: 10 minutes

Cooking Time: 20 minutes

Ingredients:

- 2 cans young green jackfruit in water, drained and shredded (20 oz, 565 g)
- 1/2 cup BBQ sauce (120 ml)
- 1 tablespoon olive oil (15 ml)
- 1 onion, thinly sliced
- 1 teaspoon smoked paprika (5 g)
- 1 teaspoon garlic powder (5 g)
- Salt and pepper to taste
- 4 sandwich buns
- Coleslaw for serving (optional)

Directions:

1. Preheat the Ninja Foodi to 375°F (190°C).
2. In a skillet, heat olive oil and sauté onion until softened. Add shredded jackfruit, smoked paprika, garlic powder, salt, and pepper, and cook for 5 minutes.
3. Stir in BBQ sauce and cook for another 10 minutes until the jackfruit is tender and the sauce is absorbed.
4. Place the jackfruit mixture in one basket and air fry for 5 minutes to caramelize slightly.
5. Serve the BBQ pulled jackfruit on buns with coleslaw, if desired.

14. Chicken Alfredo Pasta

Creamy and comforting chicken Alfredo pasta, made with tender chicken and a rich Parmesan sauce.

Servings: 4

Preparation Time: 10 minutes

Cooking Time: 20 minutes

Ingredients:

- 12 oz fettuccine (340 g)
- 1.5 lbs chicken breast, diced (680 g)
- 2 tablespoons olive oil (30 ml)
- 4 cloves garlic, minced
- 1 cup heavy cream (240 ml)
- 1 cup grated Parmesan cheese (120 g)
- 1/2 teaspoon black pepper (2.5 g)
- 1/4 teaspoon nutmeg (1 g)
- Fresh parsley for garnish

Directions:

1. Cook the fettuccine according to package instructions. Drain and set aside.
2. In a skillet, heat olive oil and cook the diced chicken until browned and cooked through. Remove and set aside.
3. In the same skillet, sauté garlic until fragrant. Add heavy cream, Parmesan cheese, black pepper, and nutmeg, stirring until the sauce thickens.
4. Toss the cooked pasta and chicken in the Alfredo sauce.
5. Serve hot, garnished with fresh parsley.

15. Greek Lemon Rice Bowls

Flavorful rice bowls topped with grilled chicken, fresh vegetables, and a tangy lemon dressing.

Servings: 4
Preparation Time: 15 minutes
Cooking Time: 20 minutes
Ingredients:

- 1.5 lbs chicken breast, diced (680 g)
- 1 cup basmati rice (185 g)
- 2 tablespoons olive oil (30 ml)
- 1 tablespoon dried oregano (15 g)
- Juice of 2 lemons
- 2 cloves garlic, minced
- 1 cucumber, diced
- 1 cup cherry tomatoes, halved (150 g)
- 1/4 cup crumbled feta cheese (60 g) (use vegan feta for a plant-based option)
- Salt and pepper to taste

Directions:

1. Cook the basmati rice according to package instructions.
2. Preheat the Ninja Foodi to 375°F (190°C).
3. In a bowl, toss the diced chicken with olive oil, oregano, lemon juice, garlic, salt, and pepper.
4. Place the chicken in one basket and air fry for 15 minutes until golden and cooked through.
5. Assemble the rice bowls by topping cooked rice with chicken, cucumber, cherry tomatoes, and crumbled feta cheese. Drizzle with extra lemon juice and serve.

16. Maple Glazed Pork Chops

Juicy pork chops glazed with a sweet and savory maple syrup sauce, perfect for a quick and delicious dinner.

Servings: 4
Preparation Time: 10 minutes
Cooking Time: 20 minutes
Ingredients:

- 4 bone-in pork chops (about 1 inch thick, 680 g)
- 1/4 cup maple syrup (60 ml)
- 2 tablespoons Dijon mustard (30 g)
- 1 tablespoon soy sauce (15 ml)
- 1 tablespoon olive oil (15 ml)
- 1 teaspoon garlic powder (5 g)
- Salt and pepper to taste

Directions:

1. Preheat the Ninja Foodi to 375°F (190°C).
2. In a small bowl, whisk together maple syrup, Dijon mustard, soy sauce, olive oil, garlic powder, salt, and pepper.
3. Brush the pork chops with the maple glaze.
4. Place the pork chops in one basket and air fry for 15-20 minutes until cooked through, flipping halfway through.
5. Serve with roasted vegetables or mashed potatoes.

17. Asian-Inspired Veggie Stir-Fry

A colorful and quick stir-fry made with a mix of fresh vegetables and a savory Asian sauce, perfect for a light dinner.

Servings: 4
Preparation Time: 10 minutes
Cooking Time: 10 minutes
Ingredients:

- 1 red bell pepper, sliced
- 1 yellow bell pepper, sliced
- 1 zucchini, sliced
- 1 carrot, julienned
- 1 cup broccoli florets (150 g)
- 2 tablespoons soy sauce (30 ml)
- 1 tablespoon hoisin sauce (15 ml)
- 1 tablespoon sesame oil (15 ml)
- 1 clove garlic, minced
- 1 teaspoon grated ginger (5 g)
- Cooked rice or noodles for serving

Directions:

1. Preheat the Ninja Foodi to 375°F (190°C).
2. In a bowl, toss the vegetables with soy sauce, hoisin sauce, sesame oil, garlic, and ginger.
3. Place the vegetables in one basket and air fry for 10 minutes until tender, shaking the basket halfway through.
4. Serve the stir-fried vegetables over cooked rice or noodles for a quick and healthy dinner.

18. Buffalo Cauliflower Bites

Crispy cauliflower florets tossed in spicy buffalo sauce, served with a side of ranch dressing for a fun and tasty meal.

Servings: 4
Preparation Time: 10 minutes
Cooking Time: 15 minutes
Ingredients:

- 1 large head of cauliflower, cut into florets
- 1/2 cup all-purpose flour (60 g)
- 1/2 cup water (120 ml)
- 1/2 teaspoon garlic powder (2.5 g)
- 1/2 teaspoon onion powder (2.5 g)
- 1/2 cup buffalo sauce (120 ml)
- 1 tablespoon olive oil (15 ml)
- Salt and pepper to taste
- Ranch dressing for serving

Directions:

1. Preheat the Ninja Foodi to 375°F (190°C).
2. In a large bowl, mix flour, water, garlic powder, onion powder, salt, and pepper to create a batter.
3. Toss the cauliflower florets in the batter until fully coated.
4. Place the cauliflower in one basket and air fry for 12 minutes, shaking the basket halfway through.
5. In a separate bowl, mix buffalo sauce with olive oil. Toss the cooked cauliflower in the buffalo sauce.
6. Return the cauliflower to the basket and air fry for an additional 3 minutes. Serve with ranch dressing.

19. Garlic Herb Roasted Potatoes

Crispy roasted potatoes seasoned with garlic and herbs, a perfect side dish for any weeknight meal.

Servings: 4
Preparation Time: 10 minutes
Cooking Time: 20 minutes
Ingredients:

- 1.5 lbs baby potatoes, halved (680 g)
- 2 tablespoons olive oil (30 ml)
- 4 cloves garlic, minced
- 1 teaspoon dried rosemary (5 g)
- 1 teaspoon dried thyme (5 g)
- Salt and pepper to taste

Directions:

1. Preheat the Ninja Foodi to 375°F (190°C).
2. In a bowl, toss the halved potatoes with olive oil, garlic, rosemary, thyme, salt, and pepper.
3. Place the potatoes in one basket and air fry for 18-20 minutes until golden and crispy, shaking the basket halfway through.
4. Serve as a side dish with your favorite main course.

20. Easy Beef Tacos

Tasty beef tacos made with seasoned ground beef, served in warm tortillas with your favorite toppings.

Servings: 4
Preparation Time: 10 minutes
Cooking Time: 15 minutes
Ingredients:

- 1 lb ground beef (450 g)
- 1 small onion, chopped
- 2 cloves garlic, minced
- 1 tablespoon taco seasoning (15 g)
- 8 small flour or corn tortillas
- Toppings: shredded lettuce, diced tomatoes, shredded cheese, sour cream, salsa

Directions:

1. Preheat the Ninja Foodi to 375°F (190°C).
2. In a skillet, cook the ground beef with onion, garlic, and taco seasoning until browned and cooked through.
3. Warm the tortillas in the second basket for 2-3 minutes.
4. Assemble the tacos by filling each tortilla with the seasoned beef and your favorite toppings. Serve immediately.

Chapter 16: Sweet Treats and Desserts

Indulge your sweet tooth with these delectable desserts that are easy to make and sure to satisfy. With the Ninja Foodi 2-Basket Air Fryer, you can create a variety of treats that are not only delicious but also healthier than traditional methods. These recipes are perfect for a quick dessert after dinner or a special treat for family and friends.

1. Air-Fried Churros

Crispy on the outside, soft on the inside, these air-fried churros are a delightful sweet treat, rolled in cinnamon sugar.

Servings: 4
Preparation Time: 15 minutes
Cooking Time: 10 minutes
Ingredients:

- 1/2 cup water (120 ml)
- 2 tablespoons unsalted butter (30 g)
- 1 tablespoon sugar (15 g)
- 1/4 teaspoon salt (1.25 g)
- 1/2 cup all-purpose flour (60 g)
- 1 large egg
- 1/2 teaspoon vanilla extract (2.5 ml)
- 1/4 cup sugar (50 g)
- 1 teaspoon ground cinnamon (5 g)

Directions:

1. In a small saucepan, bring water, butter, sugar, and salt to a boil. Remove from heat and stir in the flour until a dough forms.
2. Let the dough cool slightly, then beat in the egg and vanilla extract until smooth.
3. Preheat the Ninja Foodi to 375°F (190°C).
4. Transfer the dough to a piping bag fitted with a star tip. Pipe 4-inch strips onto a piece of parchment paper.
5. Place the churros in one basket and air fry for 8-10 minutes until golden brown.

6. In a bowl, mix sugar and cinnamon. Roll the warm churros in the cinnamon sugar mixture and serve immediately.

2. Chocolate Lava Cakes

Rich and gooey chocolate lava cakes with a molten center, perfect for a decadent dessert.

Servings: 4
Preparation Time: 10 minutes
Cooking Time: 12 minutes
Ingredients:

- 1/2 cup unsalted butter (115 g)
- 4 oz dark chocolate, chopped (115 g)
- 1/2 cup powdered sugar (60 g)
- 2 large eggs
- 2 large egg yolks
- 1/4 cup all-purpose flour (30 g)
- 1/4 teaspoon salt (1.25 g)
- Powdered sugar for dusting

Directions:

1. Preheat the Ninja Foodi to 375°F (190°C).
2. In a microwave-safe bowl, melt butter and dark chocolate together until smooth.
3. Stir in powdered sugar, eggs, and egg yolks until well combined. Add flour and salt, mixing until smooth.
4. Grease four ramekins and divide the batter evenly among them.

5. Place the ramekins in one basket and air fry for 10-12 minutes until the edges are set but the center is still slightly soft.
6. Let the cakes cool for 1 minute, then invert onto plates. Dust with powdered sugar and serve immediately.

3. Apple Cinnamon Hand Pies

Delicious hand pies filled with a spiced apple mixture, air-fried to golden perfection.

Servings: 4
Preparation Time: 15 minutes
Cooking Time: 15 minutes
Ingredients:
- 2 large apples, peeled, cored, and diced
- 1/4 cup brown sugar (50 g)
- 1 teaspoon ground cinnamon (5 g)
- 1 tablespoon lemon juice (15 ml)
- 1 tablespoon cornstarch (15 g)
- 1 package refrigerated pie crusts
- 1 large egg, beaten
- 1 tablespoon water (15 ml)
- Sugar for sprinkling

Directions:
1. In a bowl, mix diced apples, brown sugar, cinnamon, lemon juice, and cornstarch until well combined.
2. Roll out the pie crusts and cut into 4-inch circles.
3. Place a spoonful of the apple mixture in the center of each circle. Fold the dough over and crimp the edges with a fork to seal.
4. Preheat the Ninja Foodi to 375°F (190°C).
5. Brush the hand pies with beaten egg mixed with water and sprinkle with sugar.
6. Place the pies in one basket and air fry for 12-15 minutes until golden brown.
7. Serve warm with a scoop of vanilla ice cream if desired.

4. Berry Crisp

A warm and comforting berry crisp with a crunchy oat topping, perfect for any night of the week.

Servings: 4
Preparation Time: 10 minutes
Cooking Time: 20 minutes
Ingredients:
- 2 cups mixed berries (300 g)
- 1/4 cup sugar (50 g)
- 1 tablespoon cornstarch (15 g)
- 1/2 teaspoon lemon zest (2.5 g)
- 1/2 cup rolled oats (50 g)
- 1/4 cup all-purpose flour (30 g)
- 1/4 cup brown sugar (50 g)
- 1/4 cup unsalted butter, melted (60 g)
- 1/2 teaspoon ground cinnamon (2.5 g)

Directions:
1. Preheat the Ninja Foodi to 350°F (175°C).
2. In a bowl, toss the berries with sugar, cornstarch, and lemon zest. Divide the mixture among four ramekins.
3. In another bowl, mix oats, flour, brown sugar, melted butter, and cinnamon until crumbly.
4. Sprinkle the oat mixture over the berries.
5. Place the ramekins in one basket and air fry for 18-20 minutes until the topping is golden and the filling is bubbly.
6. Serve warm with a dollop of whipped cream or a scoop of ice cream.

5. Banana Bread Bites

Moist and flavorful banana bread bites, perfect for a quick snack or dessert.

Servings: 4
Preparation Time: 10 minutes
Cooking Time: 12 minutes
Ingredients:
- 2 ripe bananas, mashed
- 1/4 cup sugar (50 g)
- 1/4 cup melted butter (60 g)
- 1 large egg
- 1 teaspoon vanilla extract (5 ml)
- 1 cup all-purpose flour (120 g)
- 1/2 teaspoon baking soda (2.5 g)
- 1/4 teaspoon salt (1.25 g)

- 1/2 teaspoon ground cinnamon (2.5 g)

Directions:

1. Preheat the Ninja Foodi to 350°F (175°C).
2. In a bowl, mix mashed bananas, sugar, melted butter, egg, and vanilla extract until smooth.
3. In another bowl, whisk together flour, baking soda, salt, and cinnamon.
4. Gradually add the dry ingredients to the wet ingredients, mixing until just combined.
5. Grease a mini muffin tin and divide the batter evenly among the cups.
6. Place the muffin tin in one basket and air fry for 10-12 minutes until the bites are golden and a toothpick inserted comes out clean.
7. Serve warm or at room temperature.

6. Chocolate Chip Cookies

Classic chocolate chip cookies with a crisp edge and chewy center, made in the air fryer for a quick treat.

Servings: 4
Preparation Time: 10 minutes
Cooking Time: 10 minutes
Ingredients:

- 1/2 cup unsalted butter, softened (115 g)
- 1/4 cup granulated sugar (50 g)
- 1/2 cup brown sugar (100 g)
- 1 large egg
- 1 teaspoon vanilla extract (5 ml)
- 1 1/4 cups all-purpose flour (150 g)
- 1/2 teaspoon baking soda (2.5 g)
- 1/4 teaspoon salt (1.25 g)
- 1/2 cup chocolate chips (90 g)

Directions:

1. Preheat the Ninja Foodi to 350°F (175°C).
2. In a bowl, cream together the butter, granulated sugar, and brown sugar until light and fluffy.
3. Beat in the egg and vanilla extract.
4. In another bowl, whisk together the flour, baking soda, and salt. Gradually add to the wet ingredients and mix until combined.
5. Fold in the chocolate chips.
6. Drop spoonfuls of dough onto a piece of parchment paper and flatten slightly.

7. Place the cookies in one basket and air fry for 8-10 minutes until the edges are golden.
8. Let cool slightly before serving.

7. Air-Fried Donut Holes

Soft and fluffy donut holes coated in cinnamon sugar, perfect for a sweet snack.

Servings: 4
Preparation Time: 10 minutes
Cooking Time: 8 minutes
Ingredients:

- 1 can refrigerated biscuit dough (8 biscuits)
- 1/4 cup melted butter (60 g)
- 1/2 cup sugar (100 g)
- 1 teaspoon ground cinnamon (5 g)

Directions:

1. Preheat the Ninja Foodi to 350°F (175°C).
2. Cut each biscuit into quarters and roll each piece into a ball.
3. Place the dough balls in one basket and air fry for 6-8 minutes until golden brown, shaking the basket halfway through.
4. In a bowl, mix sugar and cinnamon.
5. Roll the warm donut holes in melted butter, then in the cinnamon sugar mixture.
6. Serve immediately.

8. Peach Cobbler

A comforting and fruity peach cobbler with a golden biscuit topping, perfect for a quick dessert.

Servings: 4
Preparation Time: 10 minutes
Cooking Time: 15 minutes
Ingredients:

- 2 cups sliced peaches (fresh or canned) (300 g)
- 1/4 cup sugar (50 g)
- 1 tablespoon lemon juice (15 ml)
- 1/2 teaspoon ground cinnamon (2.5 g)
- 1/2 cup self-rising flour (60 g)
- 1/4 cup milk (60 ml)
- 2 tablespoons unsalted butter, melted (30 g)

Directions:

1. Preheat the Ninja Foodi to 350°F (175°C).
2. In a bowl, toss the peaches with sugar, lemon juice, and cinnamon.

3. In another bowl, mix self-rising flour, milk, and melted butter until a batter forms.
4. Divide the peaches among four ramekins and spoon the batter over the top.
5. Place the ramekins in one basket and air fry for 12-15 minutes until the topping is golden and the filling is bubbly.
6. Serve warm with a scoop of vanilla ice cream.

9. Air-Fried S'mores

A fun twist on the classic campfire treat, these air-fried s'mores are gooey and delicious.

Servings: 4
Preparation Time: 5 minutes
Cooking Time: 5 minutes
Ingredients:

- 8 graham cracker squares
- 4 large marshmallows
- 4 squares of milk chocolate

Directions:

1. Preheat the Ninja Foodi to 350°F (175°C).
2. Place a square of chocolate on top of four graham crackers.
3. Top each with a marshmallow.
4. Place the s'mores in one basket and air fry for 3-5 minutes until the marshmallows are golden and puffed.
5. Remove from the air fryer and top with the remaining graham crackers. Serve immediately.

10. Pineapple Upside-Down Cake

A mini version of the classic pineapple upside-down cake, with caramelized pineapple and a tender cake.

Servings: 4
Preparation Time: 15 minutes
Cooking Time: 20 minutes
Ingredients:

- 4 pineapple rings
- 1/4 cup brown sugar (50 g)
- 4 tablespoons unsalted butter, melted (60 g)
- 1/2 cup all-purpose flour (60 g)
- 1/4 cup sugar (50 g)
- 1/2 teaspoon baking powder (2.5 g)
- 1/4 teaspoon salt (1.25 g)
- 1/4 cup milk (60 ml)
- 1 large egg
- 1/2 teaspoon vanilla extract (2.5 ml)

Directions:

1. Preheat the Ninja Foodi to 350°F (175°C).
2. In a small bowl, mix brown sugar and melted butter. Divide the mixture among four ramekins.
3. Place a pineapple ring on top of the sugar mixture in each ramekin.
4. In another bowl, whisk together flour, sugar, baking powder, and salt.
5. In a separate bowl, mix milk, egg, and vanilla extract. Gradually add the wet ingredients to the dry ingredients and mix until smooth.
6. Pour the batter over the pineapple rings.
7. Place the ramekins in one basket and air fry for 18-20 minutes until the cakes are golden and a toothpick inserted comes out clean.
8. Let cool for a few minutes, then invert onto plates to serve.

11. Air-Fried Cinnamon Sugar Pretzels

Soft pretzels coated in a sweet cinnamon sugar mixture, perfect for snacking or dessert.

Servings: 4
Preparation Time: 20 minutes
Cooking Time: 10 minutes
Ingredients:

- 1 package refrigerated pizza dough
- 1/4 cup baking soda (60 g)
- 1/4 cup sugar (50 g)
- 1 teaspoon ground cinnamon (5 g)
- 4 tablespoons unsalted butter, melted (60 g)

Directions:

1. Preheat the Ninja Foodi to 375°F (190°C).
2. Roll out the pizza dough on a lightly floured surface and cut into 8 strips. Twist each strip into a pretzel shape.
3. In a saucepan, bring 4 cups of water to a boil and add baking soda. Dip each pretzel into the water for 10 seconds, then place on a parchment-lined tray.
4. Air fry the pretzels in one basket for 8-10 minutes until golden brown.

5. In a small bowl, mix sugar and cinnamon. Brush the warm pretzels with melted butter and toss in the cinnamon sugar mixture.
6. Serve warm and enjoy.

12. Chocolate Covered Strawberries

A simple yet elegant dessert featuring fresh strawberries dipped in rich chocolate.

Servings: 4
Preparation Time: 10 minutes
Cooking Time: 5 minutes
Ingredients:

- 1 cup semi-sweet chocolate chips (170 g)
- 1 tablespoon coconut oil (15 ml)
- 1 pint fresh strawberries

Directions:

1. Preheat the Ninja Foodi to 350°F (175°C).
2. In a microwave-safe bowl, melt the chocolate chips and coconut oil together, stirring every 30 seconds until smooth.
3. Dip each strawberry into the melted chocolate, letting any excess drip off.
4. Place the strawberries on a parchment-lined tray and air fry in one basket for 2-3 minutes to set the chocolate.
5. Let the strawberries cool completely before serving.

13. Mini Cheesecakes

Creamy mini cheesecakes with a graham cracker crust, perfect for individual servings.

Servings: 4
Preparation Time: 15 minutes
Cooking Time: 15 minutes
Ingredients:

- 1/2 cup graham cracker crumbs (60 g)
- 2 tablespoons melted butter (30 g)
- 8 oz cream cheese, softened (225 g)
- 1/4 cup sugar (50 g)
- 1 large egg
- 1 teaspoon vanilla extract (5 ml)
- Fresh berries or fruit compote for topping

Directions:

1. Preheat the Ninja Foodi to 325°F (160°C).
2. In a small bowl, mix graham cracker crumbs and melted butter. Press the mixture into the bottom of four small ramekins.
3. In a separate bowl, beat cream cheese and sugar until smooth. Add the egg and vanilla extract, mixing until combined.
4. Pour the cheesecake batter over the crusts in the ramekins.
5. Place the ramekins in one basket and air fry for 12-15 minutes until the cheesecakes are set.
6. Let cool, then chill in the refrigerator for at least 1 hour. Top with fresh berries or fruit compote before serving.

14. Coconut Macaroons

Sweet and chewy coconut macaroons, lightly toasted in the air fryer for a perfect treat.

Servings: 4
Preparation Time: 10 minutes
Cooking Time: 8 minutes
Ingredients:

- 2 cups shredded sweetened coconut (170 g)
- 2/3 cup sweetened condensed milk (200 ml)
- 1 teaspoon vanilla extract (5 ml)
- 1/4 teaspoon salt (1.25 g)
- 1/4 cup melted chocolate for drizzling (optional, 60 g)

Directions:

1. Preheat the Ninja Foodi to 350°F (175°C).
2. In a large bowl, mix coconut, sweetened condensed milk, vanilla extract, and salt until well combined.
3. Scoop tablespoon-sized mounds of the mixture onto a parchment-lined tray.
4. Air fry the macaroons in one basket for 6-8 minutes until golden brown on the edges.
5. Let cool completely, then drizzle with melted chocolate if desired.

15. Baked Apples

Tender baked apples filled with a cinnamon-spiced oat mixture, a warm and comforting dessert.

Servings: 4
Preparation Time: 10 minutes
Cooking Time: 15 minutes

Ingredients:
- 4 large apples, cored
- 1/4 cup rolled oats (30 g)
- 2 tablespoons brown sugar (30 g)
- 1 teaspoon ground cinnamon (5 g)
- 2 tablespoons unsalted butter, melted (30 g)
- 1/4 cup chopped walnuts or pecans (30 g)
- Honey or caramel sauce for drizzling

Directions:
1. Preheat the Ninja Foodi to 350°F (175°C).
2. In a small bowl, mix oats, brown sugar, cinnamon, melted butter, and chopped nuts.
3. Stuff each apple with the oat mixture.
4. Place the apples in one basket and air fry for 12-15 minutes until the apples are tender.
5. Drizzle with honey or caramel sauce before serving.

16. Blueberry Muffins

Moist and fluffy blueberry muffins made quickly in the air fryer for a delicious breakfast or dessert.

Servings: 4
Preparation Time: 10 minutes
Cooking Time: 15 minutes
Ingredients:
- 1 cup all-purpose flour (120 g)
- 1/2 cup sugar (100 g)
- 1 teaspoon baking powder (5 g)
- 1/4 teaspoon salt (1.25 g)
- 1/2 cup milk (120 ml)
- 1/4 cup unsalted butter, melted (60 g)
- 1 large egg
- 1 teaspoon vanilla extract (5 ml)
- 1 cup fresh or frozen blueberries (150 g)

Directions:
1. Preheat the Ninja Foodi to 350°F (175°C).
2. In a large bowl, whisk together flour, sugar, baking powder, and salt.
3. In another bowl, mix milk, melted butter, egg, and vanilla extract. Add the wet ingredients to the dry ingredients and stir until just combined.
4. Gently fold in the blueberries.
5. Grease a muffin tin and divide the batter evenly among the cups.

6. Place the muffin tin in one basket and air fry for 12-15 minutes until a toothpick inserted comes out clean.
7. Let cool slightly before serving.

17. Air-Fried S'mores Dip

A gooey and chocolatey s'mores dip served with graham crackers for dipping.

Servings: 4
Preparation Time: 5 minutes
Cooking Time: 8 minutes
Ingredients:
- 1 cup chocolate chips (170 g)
- 1/2 cup mini marshmallows (30 g)
- 1/4 cup heavy cream (60 ml)
- Graham crackers for serving

Directions:
1. Preheat the Ninja Foodi to 350°F (175°C).
2. In a small baking dish, combine chocolate chips and heavy cream.
3. Top with mini marshmallows.
4. Place the dish in one basket and air fry for 6-8 minutes until the chocolate is melted and the marshmallows are golden brown.
5. Serve immediately with graham crackers for dipping.

18. Caramelized Bananas

Sweet and caramelized bananas served with ice cream or over pancakes for a delicious treat.

Servings: 4
Preparation Time: 5 minutes
Cooking Time: 5 minutes
Ingredients:
- 4 ripe bananas, sliced
- 2 tablespoons unsalted butter, melted (30 g)
- 1/4 cup brown sugar (50 g)
- 1/2 teaspoon ground cinnamon (2.5 g)
- Vanilla ice cream for serving (optional)

Directions:
1. Preheat the Ninja Foodi to 375°F (190°C).
2. In a bowl, toss sliced bananas with melted butter, brown sugar, and cinnamon.
3. Place the bananas in one basket and air fry for 4-5 minutes until caramelized and golden.

4. Serve warm with a scoop of vanilla ice cream or over pancakes.

19. Nutella-Stuffed Air-Fried Donuts

Delicious donuts filled with creamy Nutella, air-fried to golden perfection.

Servings: 4
Preparation Time: 10 minutes
Cooking Time: 8 minutes
Ingredients:

- 1 can refrigerated biscuit dough (8 biscuits)
- 1/2 cup Nutella (120 g)
- 1/4 cup melted butter (60 g)
- 1/2 cup sugar (100 g)
- 1 teaspoon ground cinnamon (5 g)

Directions:

1. Preheat the Ninja Foodi to 350°F (175°C).
2. Flatten each biscuit and place a spoonful of Nutella in the center. Fold the dough over and pinch the edges to seal.
3. Place the stuffed biscuits in one basket and air fry for 6-8 minutes until golden brown.
4. In a small bowl, mix sugar and cinnamon. Brush the warm donuts with melted butter and toss in the cinnamon sugar mixture.
5. Serve warm.

20. Chocolate Brownies

Rich and fudgy brownies made quickly in the air fryer, perfect for a chocolate lover's dessert.

Servings: 4
Preparation Time: 10 minutes
Cooking Time: 15 minutes
Ingredients:

- 1/2 cup unsalted butter, melted (115 g)
- 1/2 cup sugar (100 g)
- 1/2 cup brown sugar (100 g)
- 2 large eggs
- 1 teaspoon vanilla extract (5 ml)
- 1/2 cup all-purpose flour (60 g)
- 1/3 cup unsweetened cocoa powder (35 g)
- 1/4 teaspoon salt (1.25 g)
- 1/2 cup chocolate chips (90 g)

Directions:

1. Preheat the Ninja Foodi to 350°F (175°C).
2. In a large bowl, whisk together melted butter, sugar, and brown sugar until smooth.
3. Beat in the eggs and vanilla extract.
4. In another bowl, sift together flour, cocoa powder, and salt. Gradually add to the wet ingredients and mix until combined.
5. Fold in the chocolate chips.
6. Pour the batter into a greased baking dish and place in one basket.
7. Air fry for 12-15 minutes until a toothpick inserted comes out with a few moist crumbs.
8. Let cool slightly before cutting into squares and serving.

Conclusion

As we come to the end of "The Complete Ninja Foodi 2-Basket Air Fryer Cookbook," I hope you feel inspired and excited about the endless possibilities that your Ninja Foodi 2-Basket Air Fryer offers. This innovative kitchen appliance has truly revolutionized the way we cook, bringing convenience, versatility, and health-conscious cooking to the forefront of our daily routines.

The Benefits of Cooking with the Ninja Foodi 2-Basket Air Fryer

The Ninja Foodi 2-Basket Air Fryer is more than just a kitchen gadget; it's a game-changer for anyone looking to simplify meal preparation while still enjoying a wide variety of delicious, nutritious foods. Its DualZone technology allows you to cook two different dishes simultaneously, each at its own temperature and cooking time, making it perfect for busy weeknights, family gatherings, and even meal prep. Whether you're frying, roasting, baking, or dehydrating, this appliance handles it all with ease, delivering consistently excellent results.

By air frying, you can enjoy the crispy textures you love with far less oil, which means fewer calories and less fat in your meals. This makes it easier to stick to a healthy eating plan without sacrificing flavor or satisfaction. The Ninja Foodi's ability to quickly cook meals from fresh or frozen ingredients also means you can have dinner on the table in a fraction of the time it would take using traditional methods. Plus, the ease of cleaning and maintenance means more time enjoying your meal and less time scrubbing pots and pans.

Building Confidence in Your Kitchen

Cooking can sometimes feel daunting, especially when trying out new recipes or learning to use a new appliance. But with the Ninja Foodi 2-Basket Air Fryer, you've got a powerful ally in your kitchen. The recipes in this book were designed to be straightforward, approachable, and above all, foolproof. Whether you're a seasoned home cook or just starting your culinary journey, the Ninja Foodi empowers you to create meals that you and your family will love.

As you continue to experiment with the recipes provided, don't be afraid to put your own spin on them. Add your favorite spices, substitute ingredients based on what you have on hand, or even combine cooking methods to suit your tastes. The Ninja Foodi 2-Basket Air Fryer is versatile enough to adapt to your preferences, helping you build confidence with each dish you prepare.

Final Thoughts: Making the Most of Your Time and Ingredients

In today's fast-paced world, time and ingredients are precious commodities. The Ninja Foodi 2-Basket Air Fryer is designed to help you make the most of both, enabling you to cook smarter, not harder. By embracing this technology, you're not just preparing meals—you're creating opportunities to enjoy more moments with family, explore new flavors, and take care of your health.

Remember, cooking should be a joy, not a chore. The recipes in this book are just the beginning of what you can achieve with your Ninja Foodi. As you become more familiar with its features, you'll find yourself reaching for it again and again, not just because it's convenient, but because it makes cooking enjoyable and rewarding.

Thank you for joining me on this culinary journey. I hope this book has given you the tools, tips, and inspiration you need to create delicious, healthy meals with confidence. Happy cooking!

Manufactured by Amazon.ca
Bolton, ON